NELSON'S HEROES

Graham Dean

Keith Evans

THE NELSON SOCIETY

Published by the Nelson Society
Registered Charity No. 296979

ISBN O 9510702 - 5 - 8

- Contents -

Introduction

Alphabetical list of Heroes

Acknowledgements

The Heroes

- Introduction -

In the annals of naval history, no name shines brighter than that of Horatio Nelson. Monuments and memorials to him abound throughout the country, and his tomb in St Paul's Cathedral, London, is known to all Nelson admirers. But what of the men who served with the Admiral? Where are their memorials, and where do they lie? Sadly, some have no resting place other than the great oceans on which they sailed. Others lie in unmarked graves in foreign lands, and some are with their families in village churchyards, far from the sea on which they once fought so bravely. Most of the graves of these men are badly neglected. No wreaths or flowers are laid annually on their remains, and as time passes even the very stones that record their names will decay and fall, and they will be forgotten.

In this book are recorded the burial places of some of the men who served with Nelson, together with the inscriptions on their monuments and a brief biography where possible. The more famous have been omitted, as we have concentrated on the lesser known officers and men who, although in some cases they advanced to high rank, have none the less been largely passed by in Naval history.

Only men whose final resting places are known, such as the specific Churchyard or Municipal Cemetery, have been included, and where headstones have been relocated by the authorities to facilitate easier maintenance of grassed areas, the reader is informed accordingly.

With the help of Parish records and the kind permission of many a Vicar and cemetery Supervisor, we have been able to unearth and clean several of the headstones. It is hoped that, through this book, the pleasure of rescuing from obscurity many a mariner will interest readers sufficiently to look for themselves, and find the final berth of their own Nelson hero.

Any queries or discoveries are welcome, and may be forwarded to the following address: Mr G Dean
8 Wrenfield Grove
Liverpool
L17 9QD

5

Don't Pass The Salt

If you should drift upon my stone
Don't pass the salt and cast off home
Spare a thought for what it's worth
'Tis after all my final berth
Get fell in around my neck
And cat the nettles from my deck
You'll find no flowers upon my poop
No fancy vase of daffodil soup
A bird or two, maybe singing
A spider climbing in my rigging
Still here I lie run aground
My wooden hammock battened down
No more broadsides off the Cape
No more langridge, shot and grape
No more wax sealed kisses home
Nor quay-side hugs with hankies blown
The octopus roots of nearby trees
Cradle me now safe from seas
Belay a spell and keep your shirt on
I've sailed with the best from Naples to Merton
But just before you sling your hook
Log me in your spotter's book
And if it's sunny, skies not leaden
Take a photo, f.11
And if a stranger cruising past
Should ask who's that amid the grass
A Churchill, Ike or some such Nero
Tell him you've found a Nelson hero
And when you're snug with your 'Dispatch'
Knocking a grog down your hatch
Remember me, if you can
For I was once a Nelson man.

- The Heroes -

13	ALLEN, Thomas
15	ANTHONY, Charles
18	ARBUTHNOTT, Alexander Dundas Young
21	ATKINSON, Thomas
23	AUSTIN, Michael
26	BARTON, Robert Cutts
28	BLIGH, George Miller
31	BOLTON, William
33	BOWEN, Peregrine
35	BULKELEY, Richard
37	BURKE, Walter
39	BURNE, Charles
40	BURNETT, William
42	CARLETON, William
44	CARRINGTON, Noel Thomas
47	CHAPMAN, James
50	CLARK, John
52	COOKE, John
54	COOKE, Thomas Potter
55	CORLETT, Charles
57	COWELL, John
58	CUMBY, William Pryce
61	DANI, George
84	DIXIE, Alexander
86	EATON, James
88	ENTWISLE, Hugh Robert
90	EYTON, William Wynne
92	GOBLE, Thomas
93	GREENLY, John
94	HILTON, Robert & Stephen
100	JONES, Edward
101	KELLY, William
103	LAUGHARNE, William
106	LEWIS, David
108	NICHOLSON, William
109	OLIVER, John
112	PARKER, Edward Thornborough
114	PARSONS, George Samuel

118	PATRIARCHE, Charles
119	PIKE, Walter Wiltshire
121	PUDSEY, Seth
122	QUILLIAM, John
125	REEVES, Lewis Buckle
127	RIDDICK, William
130	ROTELEY, Lewis
132	RUDALL, John
133	SCOTT, John Alexander
135	SNELL, William
137	SPENCER, Samuel
138	THESIGER, Frederic
139	THOMAS, Edmund Fanning
140	TURNER, William
142	WALKER, James Robertson
144	WHICHER, John Cobb

Acknowledgements, references and sources

Austin   -   Reverend Canon Peter Absolon

Barton   -   Mr Richard Barton, Queensland, Australia

Clark   -   Reverend Griffiths, Weldon Church
                  Ron Sismey, Weldon Local History Society

Cowell   -   *Manx Worthies* by A W Moore

Greenly   -   Miss Suzanne Eward, Salisbury Cathedral
                  The Sea Chaplains by Gordon Taylor
                  Trafalgar Roll by R H Mackenzie

Hilton   -   Mrs A D M Hilton & Mr Neame

Jones   -   Mr Donald Heather, Leicester
                  Trafalgar Roll by R H Mackenzie
                  Leicester Museum & Art Gallery

Kelly   -   *Manx Worthies* by A W Moore

Nicholson -   *Wendens Ambo - the history of an Essex
                    Village* by John J Mackay
                  National Maritime Museum
                  Reverend Richard Carlile, Team Vicar in the
                  Saffron Walden Team Ministry

Quilliam   -   *John Quilliam* by Basil & Eleanor Megaw
                  JMM Dec 1942 Vol V No 67
                  Manx Worthies by A W Moore
                  Ms Hayhurst, Manx Museum

Roteley   -   Mrs Margaret Walker of Swansea

Rudall   -   The Reverend Anthony Geering
The Sea Chaplains by Gordon Taylor
The Great Gamble by Dudley Pope

Spencer   -   Registrar of Landican Cemetery, Wirral

Whicher   -   Colonel W Barttelot
The Sea Chaplains by Gordon Taylor

Text edited for publication by Mrs Sue Morris and typed by Mrs Sue Rossetti.

Photograph of Scott's tomb by Alan Pigott.

With thanks to all the Committee of the Nelson Society.

THOMAS ALLEN

Thomas Allen was born in the village of Sculthorpe, near Burnham Thorpe, Norfolk, in the year 1771. From his earliest years, Tom was in the service of the Nelson family, and when Horatio took command of the *Agamemnon* (64), Tom Allen, with others from the area, went along with the young captain to start his career in the Royal Navy. On board the *Agamemnon*, Tom was rated as Nelson's servant and accompanied him at all times. During action he would be stationed at one of the upper deck guns close to his master; on more than one occasion, when under fire, he interposed his bulky form to shield the much smaller Nelson. It is said that once during a desperate boat action, he actually placed his own head between Nelson and an attacker and received a severe wound in doing so.

Tom Allen was in charge of Nelson's personal effects, his jewels, plate, valuables, and all things belonging to him on board. He also acted as body servant, and as such, he often had to coax his little master from a wet deck and a raging storm. It has been said that he was too familiar with Nelson: on one occasion he told him off, in front of other officers, for taking an extra glass of wine, by saying, "no more now, you know it will only make you ill".

Tom was for some time at Nelson's home, Merton Place, but he did not go with the hero to Trafalgar; who knows, if he had, perhaps Nelson would have survived the battle. After Nelson's death, Tom returned to Burnham Thorpe, but without a pension of any sort he soon became very poor. He was saved from the workhouse only by the intervention of Sir Thomas Hardy, who was then governor of Greenwich Hospital. Hardy appointed him pewterer to the Hospital, and it was from this comfortable situation he was called by a very sudden death. He is buried in the old cemetery Greenwich, close to the grave of Captain Hardy. There is a fine memorial to him still standing above his grave and the inscription is as follows:

To the Memory
of
Thomas Allen
The Faithful Servant
of
Admiral Lord Nelson
Born at
Burnham Thorpe
in the
County of Norfolk
1764
and died at
the Royal Hospital
Greenwich
on the
23rd of November
1838

CHARLES ANTHONY

The main object of this work, and the research into it, was to record the names and graves of men who sailed and fought with Lord Nelson. Sadly, in some cases we are unable to photograph or record details of a grave, even though we know its site, simply because it has been moved, destroyed, or just disappeared through age. One such grave is that of Commander Charles Anthony, RN.

Commander Anthony was buried in Liverpool on August 21st 1846, in the 'Necropolis', better known as Low Hill Cemetery. This burial place was ill-conceived, being built on a bed of sandstone with very shallow top soil. As the cemetery began to fill up, things started to go wrong. It was soon decided that, because of the unsanitary conditions that prevailed there, no more burials would be made after 1898. The Corporation then decided to go ahead with a plan to remove all but the largest gravestones, and make the cemetery into a sort of park. After the removal of the stones, the ground was covered with new soil and the whole grassed over. The original walls and gateposts were left, and the site was given its new name, Grant Gardens. Today the gardens appear neglected and little used. It is somewhat strange to think that Charles Anthony still rests here in his shallow grave, while just a few feet above him, local children play their games, quite unaware of how close they are to one of Nelson's Heroes.

The records of the 'Necropolis' are now held at the Picton Library, Liverpool, and an examination of these records shows the following:

Captain Charles Anthony . R.N.
Died 18th August 1846. (Tuesday)
Interment day 21st August, 1846
Grave No. 2303. Low Hill Cemetery
Running No. 28793
Naval Commander 69 years
Cause of Death. Paralysis
Minister, Henry Hampton.

The *Liverpool Mercury*, (Deaths August 1846) gives the following short obituary:

Aug, 18th, at his residence 86, Windsor Street, Toxteth Park, in his 70th year, Commander Charles Anthony, R.N.

We also find another mention of Anthony in *Gore's Directory of 1839*:

Captain Anthony, Windsor Street, Keeper of House of Correction, Preston.

(Commander Anthony was Governor of Preston Jail from 1827-1842.)

The home of Commander Anthony has now disappeared. Windsor Street is near to the River Mersey, and the area suffered badly during the war. The work of the Luftwaffe has been finished by successive councils, and Liverpool, like many other cities, has lost much of its heritage, thanks mainly to short-sighted planners.

Despite the efforts of the planners, many of the old Georgian houses still remain in Liverpool, and some, though now in need of restoration, have been the homes of Nelson Heroes.

Charles Anthony was born in 1777 and entered the service on March 6th 1793, aged 16 years, as a first class volunteer in the *Russel* (74), under Captain John Willet-Payne. (It is said that this officer had, some years before, seduced the young Emma Hart). After participating in Lord Howe's victory of June 1st 1794, and Lord Bridport's action in 1795, he rejoined Willet-Payne in October 1796, on board the *Impetueux* (74). During the three following years, he served as midshipman and master's mate, under Sir Thomas Livingstone, Sir Home Popham, and other officers. In 1800 we find him as first lieutenant of the *Blonde* (32) in the Egyptian War. In 1801 he assisted with the disembarkation of troops at Aboukir Bay, and at the battle of Alexandria, for which he received the Turkish Medal. At Trafalgar he was a lieutenant of the *Britannia* (100), bearing the flag of Admiral Lord Northesk. After the overthrow of the combined fleets of France and Spain, he was placed in charge of

16

one of the prizes, the *Swiftsure* (74). He soon had to abandon this ship, however, in consequence of the damage she had received in the battle, and after his departure she sank with great loss of life. In 1809 he was acting captain of the *Harpy* (18) in the Walcheren Expedition, and the reduction of Flushing. In 1813 he served in the *Wolfe* (18), and commanded a division of gunboats in action with the Americans at Forty Mile Creek, and was present at the capture of two schooners. For these actions he was mentioned in despatches. In the same year he was in three actions with Commodore Chauncey's squadron, and was made up to commander. At the capture of Fort Oswego, in 1814, he was in command of the *Star* (18), and for this action was again mentioned in despatches. In December 1814, he returned to England and went on half-pay, and never returned to sea.

ALEXANDER DUNDAS YOUNG ARBUTHNOTT

Admiral Sir A D Y Arbuthnott, Kt, was the son of Lieutenant Colonel Robert Arbuthnott, 31st Foot, who died of wounds received at St Lucia in 1796. Born in Forton, Hampshire in 1789, he entered the service as boy third class in 1803, and became a midshipman in 1804. He served as midshipman in the *Mars* (74) at Trafalgar in 1805, and was at the capture of *Le Rhin* (40), 1806 and the capture of four French frigates off Rochefort by Sir Samuel Hood's Squadron in 1806. He served in the expedition to Copenhagen, 1807, and saw much gunboat service in the Baltic in 1808-9.

Promoted to lieutenant in 1809, he was in the *Impregnable* (98) at the reduction of the islands of North and South Beveland in 1811. He also served at the capture of Antwerp, and in escorting the Emperor of Russia and the King of Prussia to England in 1814. He assisted at the great Naval Review at Spithead, and was promoted to commander in 1814. He commanded the *Jasper* (10) on a mission to St Petersburg in 1823, and received the Order of St George of Russia. He was commander of the bomb ship *Terror* in the second expedition against Algiers in 1824 when he was promoted to captain. He served with the British Auxiliary Legion in Spain in 1835-37, as colonel and brigadier-general, at the relief of San Sebastian, and the storming of Irun, for which he received the honours of Knight Commander of Charles III, and the Order of San Fernando. He served in Syria in 1840-42 with the commissioners employed by the Turkish Army, which drove the Egyptian forces under Ibrahim Pasha out of Syria. He received in consequence the Turkish gold medal, and the Order of Medjidieh.

He retired as a captain in 1846, as rear-admiral in 1853, and as vice-admiral in 1858. He was knighted in 1859, and retired as admiral in 1863, receiving the Naval General Service medal and clasp. He was a Gentleman of the Privy Chamber to George IV and Queen Victoria, and died at Shenton Hall, Leicestershire in 1871.

At Trafalgar *HMS Mars* was in the lee column and sustained 98 casualties. The captain, George Duff, was one of the first killed, having his head taken off by a cannon ball. His body lay on the deck throughout the battle, covered by a Union Jack. Captain Duff asked the Captain of Marines if he thought the guns of the *Mars* could bear on the enemy ship *Fougueux* (74). The Marine officer answered 'I think not but I cannot see for the smoke.' At this, Captain Duff went to the end of the quarter-deck to look over the side. He then told his aide-de-camp, Mr Arbuthnott, to go below and order the guns to be pointed more aft. The midshipman had just turned to go with these orders when the *Fougueux* raked the *Mars* with a broadside which struck down the gallant Commander. The cannon-ball that killed Captain Duff also killed the two seamen who were immediately behind him.

The Admiral is buried in the churchyard of Shenton Church, Leicestershire. The memorial reads:

In memory of
Sir Alexander Dundas Young Arbuthnott
Admiral Royal Navy
One of the gentlemen of Her Majesty's Privy Chamber,
Knight Commander of the Order of Charles III,
and of the National and Military Order of
San Fernando of Spain;
Knight of the Imperial Order of St. George of Russia,
and the Imperial Order of the MEDJIDIEH of Turkey,
after serving his God and his country with true devotion,
died on the 8th of May 1871,
at Shenton Hall,
aged 82 years.

His remains are interred in this churchyard.

He entered the Royal Navy, April 9th 1803
Was present at the Battle of Trafalgar,
and served in the expedition before Algiers,
Accompanied the British Auxiliary Legion to Spain,
was present at the Relief of St. Sebastian,
and led the forlorn hope at the Storming of Irun.

'Not slothful in business,
fervent in spirit,
serving the Lord.'

THOMAS ATKINSON

Thomas Atkinson entered the Navy as able seaman in 1787 aged 19. His first ship was the *Colossus* (74) and within a few years he became master's mate, gaining his Master's Certificate in 1795.Whilst serving in the Channel he was transferred to the *Theseus* (74), flagship of Nelson, and was regarded as the best master in the fleet. This was the beginning of an eight-year period of service with Nelson, who took Atkinson with him from ship to ship.Thomas Atkinson served at Teneriffe, the Battle of the Nile, the siege of Acre, Copenhagen, and at Trafalgar.

Nelson's regard for Atkinson's ability was shown in a certificate he gave him in 1801, stating that he recommended 'Mr Thomas Atkinson as one of the best Masters I have seen in the Royal Navy.' Thomas amidst all of this had managed to marry Agnes, and had three sons and three daughters. The second of his sons was christened Horatio Nelson Atkinson on June 29th 1803 at St Michael-on-Wyre, Lancashire. It has often been stated that Nelson acted as godfather to Atkinson's son. However the resumption of war must have prevented Nelson's presence, as father and godfather were at sea at this date.

The name of another *Victory* officer lived on through Thomas' daughter Agnes Hardy. All three sons served in the Navy, and two of his daughters married Navy men. During the Battle of Trafalgar, as a result of the *Victory's* wheel being shot away, Thomas found himself with Lieutenant Quilliam steering the ship from the gun room by a system of rope and tackle.The log book of the *Victory* he kept after the battle remained in the family until 1911, when Sotheby's sold it on behalf of his great-grandson. It was later given to the British Museum.

On Atkinson's return to England, the artist Turner, sketching and interviewing the crew, noted that Atkinson was 'square, large, grey-eyed and 5'11".' After attending Nelson's funeral he was appointed Master-Attendant of Halifax Dockyard, Nova Scotia. He returned to Portsmouth in 1810 and finally became Master-Attendant of the Dockyard there in November 1823, where he remained until his death in 1836 at the age of 68.

An obituary appeared in the *Liverpool Mercury,* June 24th 1836, page 237, column 3:

MR. ATKINSON (MASTER OF VICTORY)

At Portsmouth in his 69th year Thomas Atkinson esq. First Master attendant. He served as Master of the Victory at Trafalgar, and of the Theseus at the Nile and was a personal favourite with Nelson. After peace had been concluded in 1803, Mr. Atkinson returned to his native county (Lancashire) and took up his residence in a village between Preston and Garstang, where he remained till the breaking out of the war, when he received a pressing communication from Nelson to resume his post on his old ship, which he complied with, and was present when Nelson met with his death.

Thomas Atkinson is buried in St Andrew's churchyard, plot 3 in Farlington, Portsmouth. He has a flat memorial stone which reads:

**TO THE MEMORY OF
THOMAS HORNBY ATKINSON LIEUTENANT OF THE
ROYAL NAVY
DEPARTED THIS LIFE 25th OCTOBER 1825 AGE 50
ALSO OF THOMAS ATKINSON ESQ LATE FIRST MASTER
ATTENDANT H.M. DOCKYARD PORTSMOUTH
WHO DEPARTED THIS LIFE THE 2ND DAY OF JUNE 1836
HE WAS MASTER OF SEVERAL OF ADMIRAL LORD
NELSON'S FLAGSHIPS INCLUDING VICTORY AT THE
BATTLE OF TRAFALGAR ALSO OF WILLIAM GEORGE
ATKINSON
LIEUTENANT R.N. GRANDSON OF THE ABOVE
INTERRED IN HASTINGS CEMETERY MAY 25TH 1914.**

Until recently sailors from *HMS Victory* have tended his grave on Trafalgar Day.

MICHAEL AUSTIN

Michael Austin first comes to light at the glorious 1st of June, where he served under Admiral Howe. He next appears as Nelson's boatswain in his flagship *Vanguard* at the Battle of the Nile where he lost an arm in the action. After spending his later years at Her Majesty's Dockyard, Chatham, Michael Austin died at his residence, Nile Cottage, Gillingham, near Chatham, Kent on June 1st 1844, aged 72. He was buried in a vault in the churchyard of St Mary Magdelene, Gillingham, Kent on June 7th 1844 and a memorial was placed in the church by his son, Horatio Thomas Austin.

The Reverend Canon Peter Absolon who helped us discover Michael Austin has kindly given the following interesting family information:

> *My great-grandmother, Maria Chambers, (née Damant) who lived in Colkirk, Norfolk and was born in 1822, used to play with the children of Mrs Girdlestone, Lord Nelson's niece, who was sister to Lady Bolton and sister also of the 3rd Lord Nelson. Maria Damant took a lead in the charades, plays and dances at the Boltons' home at Burnham, which was crammed with relics and possessions of Nelson.*

> *Lady Bolton allowed Maria to rummage among the contents of the row of chests in the long roomy attic. She said, when she was an old woman, 'Many a time I have dressed up in his uniforms and his cocked hat too. Yes, and I have run about the house brandishing his sword and thought nothing of it.' One of Nelson's great-nephews loved my great-grandmother long and hopelessly (her father would not give his consent) and he went abroad. When he came home from South Africa as an old man he visited her in Norfolk and they talked day after day of the old times they shared. Some of the Damants, however, did intermarry with the Girdlestones so I suppose I can almost qualify as a relic of Nelson!*

There are two inscriptions relating to Michael Austin.

The first, on the vault in the churchyard of St Mary Magdelene in Gillingham, Kent, reads:

Sacred
to the memory of
Thomas Fitzherbert Austin,
son of
Michael & Mary Ann Austin,
who departed this life, 28th June 1825,
aged 14 years.
Also John William Rawlinson, son of
the Revd. John Samuel Rawlinson, decd.
21st of August 1826, Aged 11 months and 13 days.
Jane Fitzherbert Austin,
Daughter of the above
Michael and Mary Ann Austin,
Died June 29th 1827 AEt. 18.
Mary Ann Austin,
Mother of the above Thomas and Jane,
Died on the 10th September 1829
Aged 51 years.
Also of George Daysh Austin,
Assistant Surgeon of H.M. Mary and member of
the Royal College of Surgeons, London,
son of the above
Michael and Mary Ann Austin,
who died 6th June 1836, aged 27 years.
Also of Mr. Michael Austin
who died 1st June 1844, aged 72 years.

The second, inside the church, is a white marble tablet, in the form of a shield, bordered by plain black marble. It is situated on the north wall of arches close to the great cross arch, and immediately below the tablet of Neil Sloman Esq. It reads:

In memory of
Michael Austin,
who died June 1st 1844,
AEtat 72,
And of Mary Anne, his Wife
who died September 10th 1829
AEtat 51.
Their remains are interred
in this churchyard.
This tablet is erected
As a mark of respect and affection
by their Son,
Horatio Thomas Austin,
The only survivor
of eight children.

ROBERT CUTTS BARTON

The son of Admiral Robert and Anna Maria Barton of Burrough House near Exeter, Devon, he was christened on December 30th 1787 at Northam, Devon. Robert Cutts Barton was one of the youngest midshipmen aboard the *Victory* at Trafalgar, yet became a lieutenant the following year in 1806.

On November 1st 1809 Commander Barton served in a cutting out expedition in the boats of the *Apollo* (38) at which four armed vessels and seven convoy ships were captured or destroyed at Rosas, off the north-east coast of Spain. Promoted to commander in 1819, he married Rebecca, daughter of Francis Lopes, by whom he had a son, Henry Charles Benyon, and two daughters, Elizabeth and Katherine Frances. Commander Barton was the last of the family to live at Burrough. Though he died in Bideford in 1827, he lies buried beneath the nave of Salisbury Cathedral not far from another Trafalgar man, the Reverend John Greenly, who rests outside.

A flat stone in the middle of the nave floor bears the inscription:

Sacred to the memory of Robert Cutts Barton
a Captain in the Royal Navy and eldest son of
Vice Admiral Robert Barton. He died on the 23rd
day of October A.D. 1827, aged 39.

The following letter written by Robert Barton after the Battle of Trafalgar is reproduced here by the kind permission of Mr Richard Barton, Queensland, Australia.

'Victory' off Cadiz
October 27th 1805

Well I know the state of anxiety you must all be in after the news of the glorious action of the 21st in which it graciously pleased the Almighty to keep me free from harm and likewise to bless His Majesty's Fleet with one of the greatest victories ever achieved. Our force consisted of twenty seven sail of the line, the combined fleet thirty three, of which nineteen were taken or destroyed. We have not heard the particulars of the engagement yet. We have suffered most severely having at one time the fire of ten ships on us at once. We had the truly melancholy sight of seeing our beloved and ever to be regretted Commander fall early in the conflict from a musket shot, and he just lived to hear the Victory was complete. Our loss is fifty six killed and eighty wounded officers and men. Our ship is very much cut to pieces and to add to our misfortunes, the night after the action we had one of the most violent gales I ever experienced which in our shattered condition made it extremely dangerous. I am afraid it occasioned the destruction of all our prizes who I am afraid were destroyed as we were on a lee shore and they all dismasted. We are now I believe making the best of our way to Gibraltar to refit a little and we shall proceed to England. Whether Admiral Collingwood will make Lord Nelson's follower or no I can not tell. In all probability I shall see you all in a month or six weeks. I shall write a few lines to my father. My watch (which I received with some other things for which I thank you all) I have lost with a gold chain and seal, as I lent it before the action to Captain Hardy's clerk, as he was stationed to minute signals, who was cut to pieces with a shot and the watch was hove overboard with him. Captain Hardy is safe and well. I have not time to say more than God Bless you all and believe me to be

> Your truly, affectionate
> Robert C. Barton
> Love and Duty to all.

GEORGE MILLER BLIGH

The son of Admiral Sir Richard Rodney Bligh, GCB, this officer entered the service in 1794 aged ten in the *Alexander* (74) commanded by his father and was aboard when it was captured by the French on November 6th 1794, after having put up one of the most heroic defences in the history of naval warfare. After suffering six months of hard captivity Bligh made his escape from Brest and returned to England on an American ship, on which Lady Anne Fitzroy, the Duke of Wellington's sister, was also a passenger.

He subsequently served in the *Brunswick* (74), *Agincourt* (64), *Quebec* (32) and *Endymion* (40) from which he was promoted in 1801 to lieutenant. He continued in the *Brunswick* until 1803. At the renewal of hostilities he was appointed to the flagship of Nelson, whose high opinion of him is reflected in a letter to his father Admiral Bligh from the *Victory* on March 19th 1804:

> *My dear Admiral, Your son is a very*
> *good young man, and I sincerely hope that,*
> *now your flag is up, you will be able to*
> *promote him. It would give me great*
> *pleasure to do it, but I see no prospect,*
> *unless we capture the whole French fleet*
> *in Toulon; therefore do you consider about*
> *him. You are sure of my regard, but I*
> *cannot kill people, and I am more likely*
> *to go off myself than anyone about me.*
> *I have many thanks to give you.*

Three days before the Battle of Trafalgar, Bligh was appointed to command the bomb-ship *Etna*, but, that vessel being absent from the fleet, he continued as lieutenant of the *Victory* and was badly wounded at his quarters on the forecastle, a musket ball striking him in the chest and passing through his left side. He appears in the painting by Devis, depicting the death of Nelson, in the cockpit below.

He was appointed Commander of the *Pylades* (16) sloop on January 25th 1806, with a convoy bound for the Mediterranean. He refused to join the *Ocean* (98) with Collingwood, not having recovered from his wound sufficiently, and he felt the Admiralty had been somewhat unfair in declining him the command of the *Etna*.

Captain Bligh continued in the *Pylades* for three further years and captured the French privateer *Grand Napoleon* on May 2nd 1808 and was promoted to post rank on December 27th 1808. He then removed to the *Glatton* (56), which at Copenhagen had been captained by his namesake, William Bligh, that much maligned commander of the *Bounty* who is believed to have been a distant relative of Captain George Miller Bligh.

Captain Bligh then moved to the *Acorn* (18), a post sloop helping in the defence of Lissa. His last appointment was on July 25th 1814, to the *Araxes* (36) frigate, from which he was paid off in July 1816. He married Miss Catherine Haynes, of Lonesome Lodge near Dorking, Surrey on December 2nd 1817. Captain Bligh died in Hampshire on October 21st 1834, aged 50, and lies in the family vault in Alverstoke church in grave no A1, the inscription of which reads:

Name	Died	Remarks
Capt. John Bligh	19.1.1795	59 years
Mrs. Ann Bligh (wife of Rear Admiral Richard Rodney Bligh and daughter of Sir Edward Worsley)	7.7.1797	52 years
Sir Richard Rodney Bligh KGCB (Admiral/Red)	30.4.1821	84 years
Capt. G.M. Bligh R.N. (Son of Rear Admiral Richard Rodney Bligh and Ann Bligh)	21.10.1834	50 years
Mary Bligh (relict of Admiral Sir Richard Rodney Bligh	4.6.1834	-
Ann Stevens (wife of Frances Stevens and sister of Capt. John Bligh and Vice Admiral Richard Rodney Bligh	8.1.1800	53 years
Frances Stevens (husband of Ann Stevens)	20.12.1807	68 years
Ann Caroline Driffield (relict of late Lt. Col. Driffield R.M. and second daughter of the late Admiral Sir Richard Rodney Bligh G.C.B.)	28.1.1843	74 years
Sophia Holmes (wife of Rear Admiral Carter and daughter of R.R. Bligh G.C.B.)	25.7.1837	61 years
Georgeanna (wife of Lt. Johnson R.N.)	6.2.1842	27 years

WILLIAM BOLTON

The lives of some of our Nelson Heroes seem to have been very ordinary, and the only thing to mark them down in history was the fact that they served or sailed with Nelson. One such person was William Bolton, of Liverpool. William is buried, along with his wife Ann, in St James' Cemetery, Liverpool. Nothing can be traced of William's life other than the fact that he served on board the *Temeraire* (98), at Trafalgar.

His gravestone states:

> *Sacred to the Memory of*
> *William Bolton*
> *Who departed this life on*
> *the 24th day of February 1850*
> *Aged 67 years.*
>
> *Deceased was one of the British*
> *Seamen who fought at the Memorable*
> *Battle of Trafalgar on Board of*
> *H.M.S. Timerara*
> (*Temeraire* spelt incorrectly).

An obituary in the *Liverpool Mercury* on Friday March 1st 1850 shows the high regard for these men, long after Trafalgar:

> *Feb 25th at the residence of his son in Rathbone Street, aged 67, Mr. William Bolton, the deceased was one of the few surviving seamen who fought at the Battle of Trafalgar on board H.M.S. Timerars* (the *Mercury* also incorrectly spelt *Temeraire*).

At Trafalgar the *Temeraire* was under the command of Captain Eliab Harvey. This 98-gun ship had, during the battle 43 men killed and a further 71 wounded, a total of 114 casualties. Only the *Victory* lost more, with 57 dead and 102 wounded.

The Fighting Temeraire, by Henry Newbolt, tells its own story of what the men on board may have thought before the battle:

> *There'll be many grim and gory,*
> *Temeraire! Temeraire!*
> *There'll be few to tell the story,*
> *Temeraire! Temeraire!*
>
> *There'll be many grim and gory,*
> *There'll be few to tell the story,*
> *But we'll all be one in glory,*
> *With the Fighting Temeraire.*

William Bolton's grave is one of the few in St James' Cemetery that has been left undisturbed. The stone, which is in good condition, is in its original place over the grave.

A few yards from the Bolton grave we find the grave of Robert Murray, 'Admiral of the White of his Majisty's Navy', (again the stone mason has made a mistake, in the spelling of Majesty) who died May 31st 1834, aged 72. Murray served mainly on the American station, and was never in action with Nelson. In this interesting graveyard we have an Admiral and an ordinary seaman within a few yards of each other - no class differences separate them now.

PEREGRINE BOWEN

Peregrine Bowen entered the Navy on January 28th 1801 as a midshipman on board the *Chapman*, a hired armed ship, under the command of Captain Robert Keen; he removed very shortly into the *San Josef* (110), under Captains Wolseley and Carpenter. From July 1803 until the year 1807, he served in the 98-gun ship the *Prince* under four different captains.

At the Battle of Trafalgar the *Prince* was under the command of Richard Grindall. Bowen was one of his midshipmen, and as such must have had a good view of the battle. *Prince* was the last ship of the lee division and had bad luck from the beginning. When the enemy were signalled she was engaged in supplying the *Britannia* (100) with water and provisions. On the morning of the battle she had split her foretopsail and had scarcely replaced it when the enemy were seen in line to leeward. She did not get into action until about three o'clock, but she made the most of her opportunities and inflicted some losses and suffered none herself. She was the only British ship to suffer no casualties during the action.

Bowen's last captain in the *Prince* was Alexander Fraser, and it was with Captain Fraser that he moved into the *Vanguard* (74), one of the ships employed with the fleet under Lord Gambier at the bombardment of Copenhagen in September 1807. In October of that year he was appointed acting lieutenant of the *Bellette* (18), under Captain John Phillimore.

He was confirmed as full lieutenant on February 23rd 1808 and moved into the *Barfleur* (98), where he acted as flag-lieutenant. From the *Barfleur*, Bowen was appointed on December 7th 1808 to the *Venus* (32), in which frigate he continued to serve at the reduction of Vigo in March 1809, and off the coasts of Spain, Portugal, Norway and Greenland, and in the West Indies, until paid off on February 14th 1814. From June 10th 1839 up to the time of his death in 1848, he was employed as Admiralty Agent in a contract steam-vessel on the Liverpool station.

Lieutenant Bowen was awarded the Naval General Service Medal with Trafalgar clasp. He died on February 23rd 1848 in London, and apparently was brought to Liverpool to be buried with his daughter in St James' Cemetery, where so many other seamen have their final berth. We see from his gravestone that, somewhat ironically, his daughter had been married to a Frenchman by the name of Braquehais from Dieppe. The gravestone (now moved from its original site) states:

To The Memory
Of
Sarah E.N.H.
the beloved wife of
N.A. Braquehais, of Dieppe, France
who departed
this life on the 23rd May 1846.
Aged 25 years.

Lieut. P. Bowen, R.N. late of
Pope Hill Pembrokeshire,
and Father of the above, died 23rd
February 1848. Aged 61 years.

Bowen's obituary in the *Liverpool Mercury*, March 3rd 1848, page 7, column 6, reads:

Feb 23.
In London aged 61, Lieut Bowen. R N One of the Admiralty Mail Masters between this port and Dublin. His remains were interred in St James' Cemetery, in this town on Monday last, 28th.

St James' Cemetery is situated in an old sandstone quarry behind the Anglican Cathedral, Liverpool. It is no longer used as a burial place and, since its reorganisation by the council, has become a place which the local youths vandalise. How times have changed.

RICHARD BULKELEY

In St John's Church, Pencombe, Hertfordshire, lies Captain Bulkeley who was a survivor of the San Juan Expedition whilst serving with the Liverpool Blues in Nicaragua. Together with Nelson, he survived the fevers of that place and kept in touch with Nelson for the rest of his life, calling on him and advising on matters of health. He was pleased to receive the Admiral when he called at his home in Pencombe whilst Nelson was on tour with the Hamiltons.

Captain Bulkeley's son, also named Richard, was present in the cockpit of the *Victory* when Nelson, hearing his voice, asked to be remembered to his father, who unfortunately died himself only six weeks after his old friend.

The following inscription is taken from a wall tablet in the church and reads:

*Under the stone below on which are the
letters R.B. are deposited in a grave
surrounded by bricks, the remains of
Richard Bulkeley Esq. late of Ludlow,
and formerley a Captain in the Army,
who died deeply lamented at the house
of his friend the Rev. J. Glasse, Rector
of this Parish.
December 15th 1805 aged 48 years.*

*Brave and sincere thy generous feeling Breast,
Mourn'd with the wretched, pitied the distrest;
Quick as the lightning flash, thy sparkling eye,
The wants of others marked with prompt supply;
Thy liberal hand, the ready gift bestow'd,
Thy manly Bosom sympathetic glow'd;
In fond rememberance, still thy image lives,
The faithful pow'r a bright resemblance gives.
Friendship records thy name with many a Tear,
Laments thy Fate, and mourns thy absence here.
Of high descent, for worth and valour famed,*

A Hero's name thy fearless Actions claimed;
Foremost in Battle, yet to Peace inclined
Retired, domestic, soft, tho' firm thy Mind.
Kindest of Husbands, Father, matchless friend,
With ceaseless Anguish o'er thy Tomb we bend.
Virtue like Thine, to Mortals rarely giv'n,
On Earth beloved, Oh may we meet in Heaven.
Best of Mankind, Farewell, thy virtuous Heart,
Now beats no more, yet tho' thy mortal Part
   In cold obstruction lies
   Swift to its native skies
   Thy angel spirit flies.

Joys everlasting crown the just above,
Then be thou blest, in Realms of Peace and Love.

     J. Yates.
     Hereford.Sculp.

WALTER BURKE

Mr Burke was purser of the *Victory* at Trafalgar when Nelson received his fatal wound and supported him till the end, as depicted in the painting by Devis. Essentially a non-combatant member of the crew, Burke was ordered by Nelson to assist below during the battle. He was the father of Commander Henry Burke who was lost in the *Seagull* in 1805, after having been wounded three times in previous actions, and of Lieutenant Walter Burke who was killed in the cutting out of the *Chevette* in 1801.

Burke lived at Wouldham, near Rochester, Kent, and was assessed for rates there in 1801. The church accounts show he was back at Wouldham in 1807 as a respected farmer 'with a touch of Nelson about him'. His prize money must have helped purchase the two buildings owned by him, 'Burke's House' and 'Purser Place'. In 1930 the latter was removed and rebuilt in Sussex. Two large shell cases which stood at his gate can be seen under the west window of the church.

Walter Burke died in Wouldham and was buried in the parish churchyard. The inscription on his headstone reads:

SACRED
TO THE MEMORY OF
WALTER BURKE
ESQ: OF THIS PARISH
WHO DIED ON THE 12th
SEPTEMBER 1815 IN THE
70th YEAR OF HIS AGE.

HE WAS PURSER ON HIS
MAJESTY'S SHIP VICTORY
IN THE GLORIOUS BATTLE
OF TRAFALGAR AND IN
HIS ARMS THE IMMORTAL
NELSON DIED.

The school in Wouldham has held a graveside ceremony annually for over 100 years and the school log book has a Victorian photograph of local children standing round the flower-decked grave on Trafalgar day.

In recent years, officers and cadets from *HMS Pembroke* have joined with the children in the Trafalgar Day ceremony which includes the reading of Nelson's original prayer.   In return the school is invited annually to visit *HMS Victory*.

CHARLES BURNE

Born in 1784, the Reverend Burne graduated with a BA at Oriel College, Oxford, in 1799. He became a chaplain in the Royal Navy in 1801 and served aboard the *Neptune* (98) at Trafalgar in 1805, under Captain Thomas Fremantle. The *Neptune* was the third ship in the weather column and exchanged broadsides with both the French *Bucentaure* (74) and the Spanish *Santisima Trinidad* (136), the largest ship in the world at that time. She lost 44 men, killed and wounded, and later towed the *Victory* to Gibraltar.

The Reverend Burne was Rector of Tedburn St Mary, Devonport from 1808 to 1852. He received his Naval General Service medal with Trafalgar clasp, and died in 1859. He was buried at St Mary's where there is a marble monument in the north aisle which reads:

Sacred
TO THE MEMORY OF THE
REVD. CHARLES BURNE
WHO DIED ON THE 24th SEPTEMBER
1859 AGED 75 YEARS.
HE WAS RECTOR OF THIS PARISH 44 YEARS
AND WAS GREATLY BELOVED AND
RESPECTED BY HIS PARISHIONERS
AND DEEPLY LAMENTED
BY HIS FAMILY AND A LARGE CIRCLE OF FRIENDS.
HE WAS SENIOR CHAPLAIN
IN THE ROYAL NAVY AND WAS PRESENT AT
THE BATTLE OF TRAFALGAR IN H.M.S. NEPTUNE
AND OBTAINED THE MEDAL
AWARDED FOR THAT MEMORABLE VICTORY.
ALSO
TO THE MEMORY OF ELIZABETH
HIS WIFE WHO DIED JUNE 22nd 1877

There is also a small floor slab in the same aisle by the organ screen. This reads:

Sacred to the memory of the Rev. Charles Burne who
died on the 24th of September 1859 aged 75 years.

SIR WILLIAM BURNETT Kt KB KCH FRS MD

This remarkable man completed his Naval service as Director-General of the Medical Department. He was born in Montrose in 1779, the son of William Burnett and entered the Navy in 1796. At the Battle of St Vincent in 1797, he served as Assistant Surgeon in the *Goliath* and also at the bombardment of Cadiz in 1797 and the Nile in 1798. In 1799 he became Surgeon of the *Athenian*, taking part in the Egyptian expedition of 1801. As Surgeon of the *Blanche* (36) he was at the capture of Cape Francois in 1803, and the operations at Curacao in 1804.

As Surgeon of the *Defiance* (74) he was present in Sir Robert Calder's action of July 22nd 1805 under Captain Philip Charles Durham, the *Defiance* being the first ship to sight the enemy. She lost eight, killed and wounded.

The *Defiance* joined Nelson on October 4th 1805 and fought in the lee column at Trafalgar. During the battle she lashed herself alongside the French 74 *Aigle* and hoisted the British colours. The French crew however, fought on and drove the boarders off. Captain Durham was obliged to cast off, and following some heavy firing the *Aigle* was finally taken. The *Defiance* also took possession of the *San Juan Nepomuceno* (74) which had struck to the *Dreadnought* (98). Her losses during the battle were 70 killed and wounded; a surgeon's duties on a day like this must have been terrible before the advent of anaesthetic and modern medicines.

Sir William Burnett became Physician, RN in 1810, Inspector of Hospitals in the Mediterranean from 1810-13 and physician to prisoners-of-war at Chatham during an epidemic of fever in 1814. He gained an MD at Aberdeen University and became an LRCP in 1825. He was knighted in 1831, and awarded the CB in 1832, becoming Director-General in 1833.

In 1835 he was Physician in Ordinary to George IV, and became an FRCP in 1836. He was the author of several scientific publications, and in 1841 the Naval Medical Service presented him with his portrait in oils and a service of plate.

For his naval service he received the Naval General Service Medal with four clasps. Sir William died in Chichester, Sussex and was buried at Boxgrove Church on February 22nd 1861. His son, the Reverend William Burnett, was vicar of that parish. There was a memorial window to him in the church, but this was destroyed by a bomb blast in 1940. Only a small portion survives in the topmost light.

WILLIAM CARLETON

This officer, the son of General Carleton, was born in America in 1790. He entered the service as a volunteer first class, in 1804. In 1805 he was a midshipman in the *Colossus* (74) at Trafalgar, under the command of Captain James Nicoll Morris. The ship joined Nelson's fleet in September, having been with Collingwood's squadron off Cadiz.

In the lee column at Trafalgar she engaged the French 74 *Swiftsure* and the Spanish 74 *Bahama*, both of which surrendered. The *Colossus* casualties were very high, with 40 killed and 160 wounded. The ship herself was also badly damaged. Apparently, during the battle, a cock flew out of the ship's hen-coop and perched on the Captain's shoulder, crowing loudly, to the amusement of the crew, bringing what must have been some light relief to the day's carnage.

After Trafalgar, Carleton became master's mate of the *Amazon* (38) and served in her boats at the cutting out of a merchantman in the Canaries, and in the capture of the French ships *Marengo* (74) and *Belle Poule* (40) in 1806. He was made lieutenant in 1810, commander in 1826, and retired as captain in 1856 with Naval General Service medal with two clasps. Captain Carleton died in 1874 aged 84 and lies buried in St Swithin, Nately Scures, Basingstoke, Hampshire.

A memorial tablet in the church reads:

In the vault of this Church are
deposited the remains of
CAPTAIN WILLIAM CARLETON R.N.
only SON of
GENERAL CARLETON
sometime governor of New Brunswick
one of the last survivors of
TRAFALGAR
he departed in the fulness of time
a brave officer
an upright gentleman
a true friend.

This tablet is inscribed to his memory
with grateful and affectionate respect
by one of the many who knew his worth
and mourn his loss.

Born 1789

Died 1874

The burial register records this entry :

No. 292 William Carleton, R.N. Hackwood Park,
Basingstoke. Buried 9th April 1874 aged 84 years.
by William M. Fletcher, Rector.

NOEL THOMAS CARRINGTON

The navy of Nelson's day attracted many a young man with its promise of adventure and foreign lands. Alas, many of their dreams were shattered in the cold light of day. One such man was Noel Carrington, born in Plymouth on July 17th 1777, the son of a grocer of some means. His father had apprenticed him at 15 to the Plymouth Dockyard when, according to his own account in the *National Biography:*

> *I was carried away by the prevailing mania and bound apprentice. I was totally unfit, however for the profession. Mild and meek by nature, fond of literary pursuits and inordinately attached to reading. Too late I repented a calling foreign to my inclinations. The ruffianism of the men sickened me.*

After having failed to change his parents' minds, he ran away, entered as a seaman on board a ship of war, and found himself suddenly at the Battle of St Vincent on February 14th 1797. This inspired the first of his poetic writings which attracted the attention of his captain who, seeing that some very untoward circumstances must have occurred to induce him to seek this line of life, sent him home.He then started teaching in Plymouth Dock and opened a school in Maidstone, Kent. One can only imagine what effect the horrors of a below-deck man-of-war must have had on the mind of a gentle and literary man.

Noel Carrington returned again to Plymouth Dock where he started an academy of schooling, by popular request, and where he remained for the rest of his days. His hours of work were seven in the morning till seven-thirty in the evening. After these hours, he composed his poetry, the first edition of which appeared in 1820.

He continued to write throughout the next ten years, though now stricken with consumption. He experienced kindness from the Duke of Bedford, Lord Russell and Sir T Acland; King George IV was a liberal patron. In July 1830 he moved to Bath with his family, but finally succumbed to consumption on September 2nd 1830. Having left instructions not to be buried in any of the 'great charnel houses of

Bath', he was interred in the little village of Combehay, four miles from Bath.

A plaque on the north wall of the interior of the church reads:

M.S.
N.T. CARRINGTON
POETAE
CUI. DULCES.IN.CARMINE.MUSAE.
NOMEN.INSIGNE.DEDERUNT.
VIXIT.DIE.II.SEPTEMBRIS.
MDCCCXXX.

AMICI:QUIDAM
VATEM.AMABILEM.HONORANDI.GRATIA.
HOC.MONUMENTUM.
POSUERUNT.

A memorial also appears in Shaugh Prior Church, Devon which reads:

SACRED
TO THE MEMORY OF
N.T. CARRINGTON

Author of "Dartmoor"; "Banks of Tamar"; "My
Native Village", and other poems.
He was born at Plymouth 17th July 1777
and died at Bath 2nd September 1830.
He lies buried in the churchyard of
Combehay near that City.
Distinguished by his literary works
He won the regard of his countrymen.
Mild and meek by nature his heart overflowed
with the "Milk of human kindness".
He loved and practised virtue
for its own pure sake and without shew of formality.
He was in spirit and in practice a humble and earnest Christian.
"Around his grave let sweetest flowers upspring
in memory of that fragrance which was once
from his mild manners quietly exhaled".

JAMES CHAPMAN

James Chapman was born in the year 1784, in the parish of Kilspindie, Scotland. He first went to sea as a boy in the merchant service, engaged mainly in the coastal trade. At the age of 22 years, while on a voyage from Scotland to London, he was pressed into the Royal Navy, and placed in the *Utrecht* (64). He was removed to the *Victory* from this ship on May 11th 1803, along with many others. He served on board this ship until after the Battle of Trafalgar, when in January 1806, he was transferred to the *Ocean* (98), Lord Collingwood's new flagship. After taking part in many actions, he was finally discharged from the service in 1814. He received the Trafalgar Medal and the Naval General Service Medal, with two clasps.

It is said that he was the last survivor of those who fought on board the *Victory*, at the battle of Trafalgar. He died on the 12th November, 1876, aged 92 years; the cause of death was given as old age.

There was an obituary in the *Advertiser* newspaper on the 13th November 1876, followed the next day by a report about the life of James Chapman, which read:

DEATH OF THE LAST SURVIVOR
OF NELSON'S VICTORY.

In our obituary column yesterday was recorded the death, in his ninety-second year, of Mr James Chapman, who was the last survivor of those who fought on board H.M.S. Victory, with Lord Nelson, at the battle of Trafalgar, on the 21st October 1805. Mr. Chapman was for some years resident at West Newport, Fife, but latterly lived at Invercarse, the residence of his son-in-law, Mr. John Earl Robertson, where he died on Sunday morning, having retained possession of his mental faculties to the last. The veteran seaman was born in the year 1784. He entered the seafaring profession while a boy, and in 1803 was pressed in the river Thames for service in the Royal Navy. From the tender he was put on board H.M.S. Victory, where he

47

served for two years under Lord Nelson, and was present with that hero at the battle of Trafalgar and in other actions. Mr. Chapman also served under Lord Collingwood, of whom he was wont to speak as being not such a disciplinarian, nor yet so well liked, as Lord Nelson was. Mr. Chapman was stroke oar in Lord Nelson's cutter; but there was no beating Lord Collingwood, he said, for that Admiral never once cast anchor during the whole of his three years' cruise on board the Ocean, 98 guns. Our veteran also served under Admiral Sir Francis Fremantle and Admiral Sir Richard Keate, and was discharged out of the Milford at the peace of 1814. Although engaged in severe actions, James Chapman received no wound, and never had any pension. He was, however, honoured with two medals - the Trafalgar Medal, with Nelson's name and words, "England expects every man to do his duty", and the Victoria Medal with two clasps, bearing "Trafalgar, October 21, 1805; Boat Service, 23rd November 1810." While resident at Newport Mr. Chapman was wont to walk up to Fergan Church until his 78th year, when he was laid down with paralysis. His speech was little affected up till the time of his death, so that he could still spin a yarn to a friend by his bedside, and the veteran passed his latter days in good cheer, and in pious trust in his God and Saviour.

On the muster books of the *Victory*, Jas Chapman is rated as lands man, this being the most inexperienced of those on board; his age is given as 22, and place of birth Edinburgh; he apparently joined the ship on 11th May, 1803, from the tender *Utrecht*.

If the muster book is correct it would appear that James, as his obituary says, may have been spinning a yarn about being Nelson's stroke oar, which would have been a job for a very experienced seaman. There is no doubt that the Jas Chapman on the muster book is James Chapman of Kilspindie. As he went to sea as a boy, by the time he joined the *Victory* he must have had a good deal of sea-going time under his belt, so it is not clear why he was rated as lands man.

James was buried from Invergowrie House, the home of his son-in-law, and was laid to rest in the Western Cemetery, on the Perth Road, Dundee. His grave, in section X1 16B, consists of a twelve-foot high arched memorial stone with kerb surround. The inscription on the stone reads:

IN MEMORY OF
JAMES CHAPMAN
SHIPMASTER, DUNDEE
WHO DIED 12TH NOVEMBER 1876
AGED 92 YEARS

ALSO OF HIS WIFE
MARGARET CRAIGIE
WHO DIED 13TH APRIL 1877
AGED 80 YEARS

AND THEIR DAUGHTER
ANN CHAPMAN
WIFE OF JOHN EARL ROBERTSON
WHO DIED 15TH APRIL 1908
AGED 77 YEARS

THE ABOVE
JOHN EARL ROBERTSON
DIED 11TH JANUARY 1919
AGED 86 YEARS.

JOHN CLARK

Reading through a book called 'The King's England' by Arthur Mee, I was interested to see a mention of Weldon Church, Northamptonshire. It was stated that the west window of this church was once owned by Admiral Lord Nelson, and was given by him to Sir William Hamilton. As a member of the Nelson Society, I was of course very interested in this, especially as we had no record of it in our files. Another link with Lord Nelson was also mentioned: a tablet in the south aisle to the memory of Doctor John Clark, who took part in the Battle of Trafalgar and was for 45 years doctor of the village of Weldon.

The Nelson window, as we shall call it, is of 16th- or 17th-century Flemish stained glass and depicts the Adoration of the Magi. It shows the Wise Men kneeling at the manger, with Ethiopian slaves in gorgeous dress, decked with jewels and wearing rings in their ears, bringing forward offerings of gold and silver.

The inscription below the window states that it was given by Lord Nelson to Sir William Hamilton. The window was presented to Weldon Church in 1897 by the Reverend William R Finch-Hatton, whose father had inherited a number of Sir William Hamilton's effects. Despite researching the Hamilton papers and wills, we can find no mention of the window. It is the general opinion of the Nelson Society that the window was a trophy of war, taken by Nelson, possibly at the Battle of the Nile, and presented to Sir William Hamilton who was an avid collector of such things.

The east window of Weldon Church is also of interest to the Nelson Society because it was given by Doctor John Clark in 1860, just three years before his death. The inscription in the window reads:
In honour of God this window is dedicated AD MDCCCLX by John Clark surgeon of this place 44 years who was 12 years in the Navy and served at the Battle of Trafalgar.

At Trafalgar, John Clark served as surgeon's mate, in HMS *Dreadnought* (98), under Captain John Conn. The master was a man named Richard Burstal and the surgeon, William Dwyer. *Dreadnought* was the tenth ship in the lee column under Vice-Admiral Collingwood, and she engaged the enemy an hour and 13 minutes after the start of battle. During the battle she had six seamen and one marine killed; one officer, two petty officers, 19 seamen and four marines wounded, a total of 33 casualties. In 1808 John was made a full surgeon and was awarded the Naval General Service Medal with Trafalgar clasp. He later retired from the Navy to Weldon, where he died on July 1st 1863 aged 77 years.

JOHN COOKE

There must have been many a man who survived the horrors of war only to die in an accident at home. One such unfortunate was Lieutenant John Cooke. It is hard to contemplate a sadder ending for a brave and gallant officer than that which befell John Cooke.

The circumstances of his death were given in the *Nottingham Journal* printed on Friday, October 29th 1813. It states:

> *On Tuesday last, Lieutenant John Cooke of the Royal Navy, an officer of tried gallantry and great nautical experience, who had served his country in seventeen different actions and particularly at the ever-memorable Battle of Trafalgar. The circumstances attending his death were of a nature peculiarly afflicting: he went out on Monday morning on a shooting excursion, in the liberties of Wilford in company with a relation and in passing through a hedge, the piece of the latter accidentally went off and lodged the whole contents in Lieut. Cooke's body. Surgical aid was immediately procured but the wound was too desperate to admit of relief and he died the following day. This most unfortunate and lamentable catastrophe has involved his friends in the deepest affliction.*

The obituary gives the date of his death as October 26th in contrast to October 27th on his headstone. His age on the headstone also differs from that given in the Parish register, which reads as follows:

> *NAME.*   John Cooke a Lieutenant in the
>   Royal Navy
> *ABODE.Arnold*
> *BURIED.*   October 28th 1813 Age 41.

Arnold was then a village with its parish, situated about four miles north of Nottingham. He was buried in the churchyard of St Wilfrid's Church, Wilford, near the east window.

The inscription on his headstone states:

Erected
to the Memory of
Lieut John Cooke
late of his M.S. Ville de Paris;
He died 27th Oct 1813
AGED XXXIX YEARS

How sudden and how awful was the stroke,
By which the slender thread of life was broke;
O may this admonition teach us all,
How frail is man, how unforeseen his fall.

At the Battle of Trafalgar, John Cooke served on board the *Defence* (74), under Captain George Hope. This ship was in Collingwood's column, near the rear, and although she was closely engaged came out of the action quite well with only seven killed and a further 29 wounded. It is remarkable that no officers were among the casualties.

Lieutenant Cooke's abode is given as Arnold, yet we find him buried in the churchyard at Wilford, a district to the south of the city of Nottingham. We must assume that he was on a visit to his family when the tragic accident happened, and indeed his obituary states that he was with a relative at the time of the accident. We have noticed that the grave to the left of John's also belongs to members of the Cooke family. In years gone by, St Wilfrid's would have been considered a country church, with the River Trent winding its weary way past. Now the church stands in a sprawling suburb of Nottingham.

THOMAS POTTER COOKE

Cooke was born on April 23rd 1786, in Titchfield Street, Marylebone, where his father, whom he lost when aged seven, practised as a surgeon. Watching a nautical melodrama inspired Cooke to go to sea. In 1796, at the age of ten, he sailed in the *Raven* (18) and was at the siege of Toulon. In 1797 as boy third class, he was present at the Battle of St Vincent still on the *Raven* captained by W Prowse.

He was shipwrecked off Cuxhaven and was rescued after taking refuge in the rigging. Upon reaching England he joined the *Prince of Wales* (98), which was carrying Rear-Admiral Sir Robert Calder to the blockade of Brest. The peace of Amiens, in 1802, seems to have ended his naval life and in 1804 he began his stage career at the Royalty Theatre in Wellclose Square.

Cooke then appeared as Nelson at the Amphitheatre, and continued treading the boards at such theatres as the Lyceum and Drury Lane. He appears to have made a great success at the Lyceum as Frankenstein, the hero of *The Vampire,* and he played Long Tom Coffin in Fitzball's drama *The Pilot.* He played 80 successive nights at the Porte-Saint-Martin, Paris in 1825.

In 1827 he was seen at Edinburgh by Christopher North who damned him with faint praise, alluding to him as 'the best sailor out of all sight and hearing that ever trod the stage.'

His last appearance was at Covent Garden, on October 29th 1860 in *Black-eyed-Susan.*

He died on April 10th 1864, at 37 Thurloe Square, the house of his son-in-law, and was buried at Brompton Cemetery. He left £2000 to the masters of the Dramatic College, the interest of which was to be paid for a prize Nautical Drama. He received his Naval General Service medal and clasp for his service at the Battle of St Vincent.

CHARLES CORLETT

On the headstone of Charles Corlett, the inscription has now all but gone, but it should read:

> *One of Nelson's Hero's*
> *Thy Will*
> *be done*
>
> *In Memory of*
> *Charles Corlett*
> *Armourer of H.M.R.N.*
> *Who Departed this Life on*
> *The 25th January 1862 Aged 91 years.*

Little is known about Charles Corlett. He was born on the Isle of Man in the year 1771, and after his naval career lived in Tranmere, Wirral, along with his family. It is obvious that his next of kin were very proud of the fact that he had served in Nelson's fleet by the care taken in the design of his gravestone at St Andrew's, Bebington.

It is interesting to note that the area in which the churchyard stands is called Trafalgar.

Charles Corlett's obituary appeared in the *Liverpool Mercury* on February 1st 1862 and gives us some details of his naval service. It states:

> *CORLETT - Jan. 25, at the residence of his son, No. 7, Wellington Street, Rock Ferry. Mr. Charles Corlett, aged 91. The deceased was one of Admiral Lord Nelson's heroes, and was at the Battle of the Nile 1798, Copenhagen 1801, Trafalgar 1805. Was at the siege of Rangoon, in the East Indies; was in several cutting out expeditions, and was several times taken prisoner and made his escape; and what is remarkable, the deceased only received one shot wound in the thigh, during the whole of his career.*

On Wednesday last the deceased was interred with all naval honours by kind permission of Capt. Inglefield, of Her Majesty's ship, MAJESTIC, about 60 of the crew, consisting of marines, seamen, naval volunteers in procession, bearing him to the graveyard, Bebington, on a fieldpiece belonging to the ship.

N.B.
The siege of Rangoon took place in 1824. One of the vessels involved, *HMS Larne*, was commanded by the famous author of sea tales, Captain Marryat.

HMS Majestic was on coastal Protection service in 1862 and was visiting the port of Liverpool.

JOHN COWELL

John Cowell was born in 1786. He lost his right arm at Trafalgar, and died in 1863. He is buried at St Bridgett's Kirk, Bride, Isle of Man. The following is taken from 'Manx Worthies' by AW Moore:

The son of a northside farmer, John Cowell was carried off by a press-gang from Douglas and became one of the crew of the *Temeraire* (98), on board which ship he lost his right arm, by a cannon shot which struck him just as he was in the act of ramming home a cannon charge. On his return home, duly pensioned, he became a student, acquiring a knowledge not only of navigation and the Manx language, but also of science and the classics. Notwithstanding his physical disability he was invited to enter the Ministry of the Wesleyan Methodist Church, but he preferred the profession of a schoolmaster. He was also a land surveyor, and he conducted a survey of the island for the English Government.

As a lay preacher he was both able and eloquent. For many years he was parish clerk of Bride, thus uniting, like many of the early Wesleyans, service in the Church of England with fidelity to his own denomination. On one occasion his zeal in holding religious meetings brought him into collision with the archdeacon, who complained to the Bishop. The latter, who thereupon summoned him to Bishop's Court, on finding that he was well versed in the old English divines and was able to give reasons for his faith and to make it clear to others, sent him away with his blessing, telling him to continue his good work.

During the epidemic of cholera at Dalby, he distinguished himself by his tender care of the sufferers whom others shunned. We may mention that he was a brother-in-law of William Kennish, that several of his grandsons are now in the Wesleyan ministry and one Mr. J.T. Cowell is a Justice of the Peace and a member for Douglas in the House of Keys. Endowed with real genius, John Cowell was also a man of the highest character and he has left an honourable name behind him. He died in 1863.

WILLIAM PRYCE CUMBY

The son of Captain David Pryce Cumby, by his first wife, Eleanor of Heighington, County Durham, he is recorded as having been born in Dover, on March 20th 1771, although Heighington, County Durham regard him as their own.

Captain Cumby entered the service in May 1784 as a midshipman aboard the *Kite* cutter, employed against the smugglers on the north-east coast of England. After a period in the merchant service, he joined the *Brazen* cutter and passed his lieutenant's examination in March 1792, before sailing to the Newfoundland station in the *Assistance* (50). In June 1799 he began a three year period as flag-lieutenant to Vice-Admiral Graeme, Commander-in-Chief in the Medway.

At the renewal of hostilities in May 1803, Cumby took command of the *Swift* (18) cutter, and was then appointed to the Norfolk Sea Fencibles in May 1804. In November he became first lieutenant of the *Bellerophon* (74), under Captain John Cooke, in which position he served with distinction at Trafalgar.

Early in the battle the *Bellerophon* was engaged with the *Monarca* (74) and *L'Aigle* (74), when Captain Cooke was mortally wounded whilst re-loading his pistols. He had just given Cumby orders to go below to direct the lower deck, and the Lieutenant found on his return that his Captain had been shot in the chest, a musket ball having broken two ribs and passed through his lungs. His last words were 'Let me lie one minute'.

It had always been Captain Cooke's dearest wish to serve in a general engagement with Nelson which would, he said, crown all his military ambition. As events transpired he was granted his wish, and remarkably he fell at the same time, and almost in the same manner, as the man he so much admired.

Cumby now succeeded to the command and, after some fierce exchanges, he compelled the *Monarca* to surrender. On the *Bellerophon* 150 men were killed and wounded. The *L'Aigle*, which had disentangled herself, lost nearly two-thirds of her crew.

On his return to England, Cumby was promoted to post-captain, and he attended Nelson's funeral in the January of 1806. In June 1809 Captain Cumby in the *Polyphemus* (64) commanded a squadron sent from Port Royal, and captured the city of St Domingo on the Jamaica station.

Captain Cumby married first Miss Metcalf in 1801 and secondly, Elizabeth Morley in 1818. He had three sons and a daughter.

He returned to live in Heighington, Durham, after the war, and built a home known as Trafalgar House from his prize money. He finally became Superintendant of Pembroke Dockyard in 1837, where he died, on September 27th 1837. He was buried in St Mary's churchyard, Pembroke on October 5th 1837, entry No. 659, aged 67 years. The graveyard has recently been cleared and transformed into a lawned garden, with only a few slate stones remaining to one side.

In St Michael's Church, Heighington, Durham, there is a memorial to Captain Cumby which reads:

SACRED TO THE MEMORY OF
CAPTAIN WILLIAM PRYCE CUMBY R.N.C.B.
WHO DIED AT PEMBROKE
CAPTAIN SUPERINTENDANT OF THE NAVAL ARSENAL
AND IN COMMAND OF THE ROYAL SOVEREIGN YACHT
XXVII SEPTEMBER MDCCCXXXVII AGED LXVI
IN THE BATTLE OF TRAFALGAR
WHERE AT AN EARLY PERIOD OF THE ENGAGEMENT
HE SUCCEEDED TO THE COMMAND OF THE
"BELLEROPHON" OF 74 GUNS WHICH WAS THEN
OPPOSED IN THE HOTTEST OF THE ACTION TO A
SUPERIOR FORCE BEING IN CONTACT WITH THE
FRENCH
SHIP L'AIGLE CLOSELY ENGAGED WITH THE SPANISH
SHIP EL MONARCA AND EXPOSED TO THE FIRE OF
SEVERAL OTHER SHIPS OF THE ENEMY'S LINE
HE NOBLY MAINTAINED THE UNEQUAL CONTEST
DISPLAYING IN THIS CRITICAL POSITION
A SKILL AND VALOUR WORTHY OF THE EVENTFUL DAY
AND ANIMATING BY HIS EXAMPLE
THE VICTORIOUS EFFORTS OF HIS GALLANT CREW.
AT THE CAPTURE OF THE CITY OF ST. DOMINGO
HE ACQUIRED ADDITIONAL DISTINCTION
BY THE GREAT ABILITY WITH WHICH HE CONDUCTED
THE OPERATIONS OF THE NAVAL FORCE
AND BY HIS HUMANITY TO THE VANQUISHED
ON THEIR SURRENDER TO THE BRITISH ARMS
IN HIS PROFESSION
HIS CONSIDERATE CARE FOR THE COMFORTS
OF THOSE UNDER HIS COMMAND
SECURED TO HIM THE SERVICE OF ATTACHED HEARTS,
IN PRIVATE LIFE HIS CHEERFUL TEMPER AND SOCIAL
KINDNESS ENDEARED HIM TO ALL CLASSES
IN AND AROUND THIS VILLAGE
WHERE HIS VIRTUES AND UNAFFECTED PIETY
DIFFUSED THE CALM ENJOYMENTS OF DOMESTIC
PEACE
OVER HIS HAPPY HOME.

VIRTUE ET OPERA

GEORGE DANI

At the Battle of Copenhagen, amidst the fury of a most violent conflict between the Danes and a British Fleet under the command of Sir Hyde Parker, Nelson very calmly wrote his celebrated letter to the Danish Crown Prince. He insisted on meticulously sealing the document with candle and sealing wax, to avoid any appearance of undue haste. A romantic Victorian woodcut shows Lord Nelson sealing his renowned letter to the Danish Crown Prince. In fact the letter was written on the quarter-deck of the *Elephant* (74), using the rudderhead casing as a table. The ship was still in action and the first man sent for candle and wax was killed. The seaman who actually held the candle for Lord Nelson on this occasion was George Dani.

He was born in the year 1776 and was a native of Pisa in Tuscany. He left home at the early age of 11 to go on board a British man-of-war and he remained in the service until 1806. He served under Sir John Jervis and Lord Nelson, and was present at the Battles of St Vincent, the Nile and Copenhagen. He was afterwards engaged in the service of the City of Dublin Steam Packet Company, and was for upwards of 25 years their respected servant, only retiring three years before his death in 1856. He received a gold medal for meritorious aid to those on board the burning ship *Ocean Monarch,* off the Great Ormes Head in August 1848, and also for his previous naval engagements.

George Dani died on November 28th 1856 at his residence, 30, Brunel Street, Liverpool. (His residence, like Nelson's, no longer stands.) He was interred in St James Cemetery, Liverpool, in a grave already occupied by his wife, Mary Anne, who died ten years before him. His death certificate states that he was 80 years old and that the cause of death was 'disease of the heart, 3 years certified', it also tells us that his occupation was 'Master Mariner'. The informant is given as G. Dani, presumably his son, who lived at 2, North Street, Toxteth Park, Liverpool.

Dani's headstone incorrectly gives his age as 75 years. It has been moved from its original site and has become somewhat damaged. St James Cemetery, like so many others, has been rearranged by the local council in order to make it easier to maintain. Many gravestones have been damaged and some lost for ever, but along with Dani, we have found five more of Nelson's Heroes in this place: the reader will find them mentioned elsewhere in this publication.

The obituary of George Dani appeared in the *Liverpool Daily Post*, Tuesday 2nd December 1856. It reads:

> *On the 28th November 1856, at his residence Brunel St. Everton. Captain George Dani. Deeply regretted. He fought with Nelson at the battles of the Nile, Copenhagen and St Vincent. He was also for many years in the service of the City of Dublin Steam Packet Company.*

It is stated earlier that Dani had received a gold medal for giving aid to the passengers and crew of the burning ship *Ocean Monarch* and the following extract from the *Liverpool Mercury* for August 29th 1848 shows the brave seaman acting as one would expect:

> *The following is a correct statement from Captain G. Daney* (his surname is spelt incorrectly) *of the City of Dublin Steamer 'Prince of Wales' who, seeing the distressed situation of the 'Ocean Monarch' while on his passage from this port to Beaumaris, in the most praiseworthy manner, bore down towards her and was happily the means of saving the lives of a large number of passengers. After the gallant captain and his crew had rendered all the assistance in their power and had seen the last people taken from the wreck, the steamer, having some of the people on board who were saved by their humane exertions, proceeded to her destination where she arrived at 8 o'clock.*

> *Captain Daney's Statement.*

> *When outside the lightship I discovered a ship on fire, bearing about 12 miles N.W. I immediately hauled up for her and ordered one of the boats to be got ready, in going along I*

discovered a boat with four hands in it. I took her in tow and in a short time after I saw a man floating on a part of the wreck. I sent a boat to pick him up and got him on board. At this time there was a great deal of the wreck floating about. I lowered my boat and sent Mr. Batty, the mate, and three hands to see if they could pick up anyone alive. As Mr. Batty was going into the boat, he discovered the body of a child not quite dead, but it was too far gone to recover. I then proceeded to the ship on fire and got three more passengers that were floating. When I came up to the ship she was in one flame from fore to aft. I did not think it prudent to go alongside of her but I came to anchor close ahead of her. At this time the wind was increasing and a heavy sea running, and so much of the wreck hanging about the vessel the boats could not approach her in safety. I then got the passengers to assist me to weigh anchor and returned to pick up my own boat. I then returned to the ship and saw from twenty to thirty people under the bowsprit of the ship. I then came to anchor close on her starboard bow and got lines attached to the boats and saved everyone that was left on the wreck.

At this trying moment Mr. Batty was of the greatest service to me as well as all other hands who cheerfully and willingly assisted me in saving all they could.

Tom Allen

Alexander Arbuthnott

William Bolton

SACRED to the MEMORY
of
WILLIAM BOLTON,
who departed this life on
2nd of February 1850
Aged 67 Years,
Deceased was one of the British
Spanien who fought at the Memorable
Battle of Trafalgar on Board of
H.M.S. Tonnerare,
ALSO of ANN BOLTON, Relict of

Walter Burke

James Chapman

NEAR TO THIS STONE
ARE THE MORTAL REMAINS OF
JOHN CLARK
FORMERLY OF HER MAJESTY'S NAVY
AND FOR THE LAST 45 YEARS OF HIS LIFE
SURGEON IN THIS PARISH
HE DIED JULY 1 1863
AGED 77 YEARS

John Clark

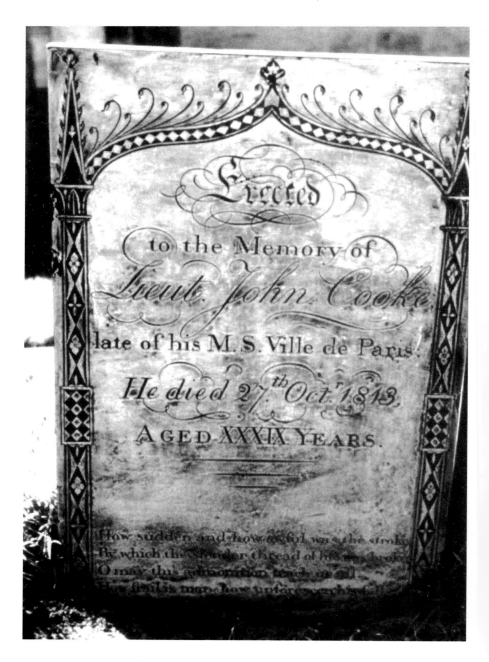

Erected

to the Memory of

Lieut. John Cooke

late of his M.S. Ville de Paris.

He died 27th Oct. 1813,

AGED XXXIX YEARS.

How sudden and how awful was the stroke
By which the slender thread of life was broke
O may this admonition teach us all
How frail is man, how unforeseen his fall.

John Cooke

Charles Corlett

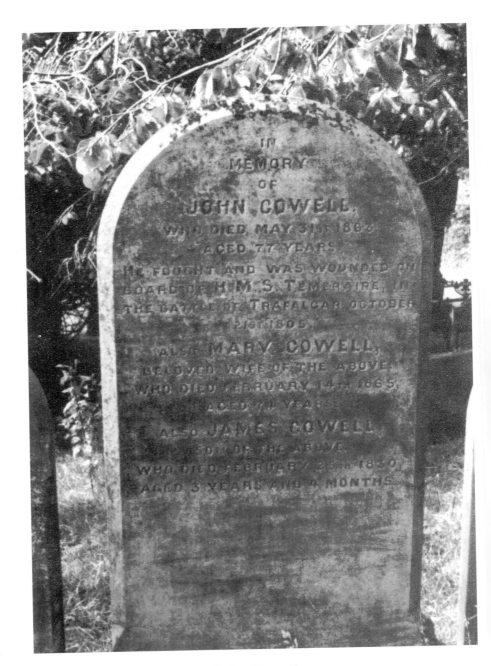

IN
MEMORY
OF
JOHN COWELL,
WHO DIED MAY 31st 1863
AGED 77 YEARS.
HE FOUGHT AND WAS WOUNDED ON
BOARD OF H.M.S. TEMERAIRE, IN
THE BATTLE OF TRAFALGAR OCTOBER
21st 1805.
ALSO MARY COWELL,
BELOVED WIFE OF THE ABOVE,
WHO DIED FEBRUARY 14th 1865,
AGED 78 YEARS.
ALSO JAMES COWELL,
SON OF THE ABOVE
WHO DIED FEBRUARY 25th 1830,
AGED 3 YEARS AND 4 MONTHS.

John Cowell

James Eaton

Hugh Entwisle

**Lady Hamilton's Baptism Font
Neston Church. (See William Snell.)**

STOP, TRAVELLER, STOP, AND READ

This Stone was Erected by those
who fully Appreciated the integrity
and fidelity of *DAVID LEWIS*
alias *the old Commodore* who
departed this life on the
16th day of Feby 1850,
AGED 66 YEARS.

He nobly fought on board the Conqueror
under *NELSON* at the battle of *Trafalgar*
and for the last 15 years perform'd
Zealously the duties of deputy
Harbour Master at this Port.

Here lies *David Lewis* what then
Dust: when his Master calls will rise again

David Lewis

Walter Pike

John Quilliam

Lewis Buckle Reeves

Lewis Roteley

Alexander John Scott

William Snell

SACRED.
to the memory of
SAMUEL SPENCER Esq.
Lieut. R.N.
who departed this life
Dec.r 19th 1850
Aged 71 Years.
ALSO
CHARLOTTE MATILDA SPENCER
second daughter of the above
who departed this life
March 6th 1870.

Samuel Spencer

83

SIR ALEXANDER DIXIE Bart DL JP

Third son of the Reverend Beaumont Dixie and Margaret, daughter of Richard Shewin, this officer was born in 1780 and entered the service as a volunteer first class in 1795. He was unfortunately wrecked in the *Amazon* (36) and taken prisoner in the action with the French 74, *Les Droits de l'Homme* in 1797. He served as a midshipman in *La Pomone* (40) in the Holland expedition in 1799 and was made lieutenant in 1804.

At Trafalgar, Alexander Dixie was third lieutenant of the *Phoebe* (36) under Captain Hon Thomas Bladen Capel, the frigate bringing valuable service to Nelson as one of the 'eyes of the fleet'. She was to windward of the weather column but took no part in the actual engagement. The *Phoebe*, however, saved the French *Swiftsure* (74) and later brought out the *Bahama* (74).

One of Dixie's fellow lieutenants aboard the *Phoebe*, Lieutenant Hindmarsh, was one of only three people to have received seven clasps to his Naval General Service medal.

Lieutenant Dixie was promoted to commander in 1814. In the *Saracen* (18) he captured and destroyed several vessels in the Chesapeake during 1814 and 1815. He succeeded to the Baronetcy in 1850, and retired from the Navy in 1851, having received two clasps to his Naval General Service medal in 1848.

Captain Dixie died at Bosworth Park in 1857 and is buried in St Peter's churchyard, Market Bosworth, Leicestershire. His ivy-clad stone, in the form of a sarcophagus with anchor and rope entwined, bears the inscription:

In memory of
Capt. Sir Alexander Dixie Bart.
who departed this life
on the 20th day of December A.D. 1857
in the 78th year of his age.

"Be ye ready for in such an hour as ye think not the son of man cometh"

Matthew.

"What man is he that liveth and shall not see death"

In All Saints' Church, Cadeby, a few miles from Market Bosworth, there is a fine wall memorial to Captain Dixie with the beautiful verse from Ephesians IV.32.

Be ye kind one to another, tender hearted,
forgiving one another, even as God for
Christ's sake hath forgiven you.

JAMES EATON

Commander Eaton was born in London in 1786 and entered the service in 1799. He was in the *Hannibal* (74) when she had to surrender in the action off Algeciras in 1801. He was midshipman in the *Atalante* (16), cutting out vessels near St Gildas in Quiberon Bay in 1803.

He served as signal midshipman of the *Temeraire* at Trafalgar, where, as stated on his headstone:

> ***He had the honour of repeating***
> ***from the "Victory" Nelson's***
> ***last immortal signal; England***
> ***expects that every man this day***
> ***will do his duty.***

The *Temeraire* (98), under Captain Eliab Harvey, was second ship in the weather line behind the *Victory*. She had a particularly fine role in the battle, coming to the *Victory's* aid at a crucial stage. At one time she had both the *Redoutable* (74) and *Fougueux* (74) close alongside. The latter was boarded by 28 men under Lieutenant Kennedy and, after a ten minute fight to the main mast, they succeeded in hoisting the British colours.

The *Temeraire's* losses were 121 killed and wounded, and a further 43 were lost when prizes foundered in the following storm. Of the ship's conduct in the fight, Collingwood wrote 'I have no words in which I can sufficiently express my admiration of it.'

As she was being towed to the breakers at the end of her career, the artist Turner saw her whilst boating with friends, and the idea for his famous painting 'The Fighting Temeraire' was born.

James Eaton was promoted to lieutenant in 1806, and was wounded when taking a convoy to China in the *Lion* (64). He was present at the reduction of Java in 1811, and distinguished himself in rescuing the crew of a Swedish vessel in 1813.

His house still stands in Dagger Lane, West Bromwich and has recently been renovated. He retired as commander in 1842, with a medal and two clasps, and died in 1857.

Commander James Eaton was buried in All Saints' churchyard, West Bromwich and his headstone can be seen near the main door. Its inscription reads:

SACRED TO THE MEMORY OF
CAPTAIN JAMES EATON R.N.
OF HILL HOUSE, WEST BROMWICH
WHO DIED ON FEBRUARY 28th 1857
AGED 71 YEARS.
HE WAS A GALLANT OFFICER AND AN
AFFECTIONATE HUSBAND.
HE WAS SIGNAL MIDSHIPMAN
AT THE
BATTLE OF TRAFALGAR OCT. 21st 1805
AND HAD THE HONOUR OF REPEATING
FROM THE VICTORY
NELSON'S LAST IMMORTAL SIGNAL:
ENGLAND EXPECTS THAT EVERY MAN
THIS DAY WILL DO HIS DUTY.

R.N.A.

HUGH ROBERT ENTWISLE

The son of John Markland of Foxholes, Rochdale, who assumed the name of Entwisle. Born in 1785, this officer joined the Navy in 1799, aged 14. He served in the *Amethyst* (36) commanded by his relative Captain John Cooke, and was present at the capture of *La Dédaigneuse* (36) and *Le Général Brune*, in 1801.

He was rated A.B. although he served as a volunteer first class aboard the *Bellerophon*, under Captain Cooke, at Trafalgar, together with his cousin John Edward Markland, who was also a volunteer. During the battle, he was one of the party who took possession of the *Bahama* (74). He was promoted first lieutenant to the *Paulina*, a sloop of 16 guns on January 28th 1806, sailing on its first cruise on March 26th under Captain Lumley.

Commander Entwisle was present at the expedition to Copenhagen in 1807, and served in the *Bucephalas* (32) at New Orleans in 1814.

In 1824 he married Mary Anne, eldest daughter of James Royds of Rochdale. He retired as commander in 1839, with a medal with one clasp, and died in 1867 aged 82.

Commander Entwisle lies buried in Llanblethian churchyard, South Glamorgan, with his wife and next to his brother and sister.

His headstone reads:

SACRED

To the memory of Hugh Robert, 2nd
son of John Entwisle Esq. of Foxholes
in the County Palatine of Lancaster,
Commander in the Royal Navy.
D.L., J.P. for the County of Glamorgan
Who died at Marlborough Grange
23rd December 1867. Aged 82
Dearly beloved

In the church there is also a wall memorial to the Entwisles, which reads in part:

HUGH ROBERT, 2nd SON OF THE ABOVE
JOHN ENTWISLE, A DEPUTY LIEUT. & J.P. FOR
THE COUNTY OF GLAMORGAN, COMMANDER IN THE
ROYAL NAVY, PROMOTED AS LIEUT. & RECEIVED A
MEDAL FOR HIS SERVICES AFTER THE BATTLE OF
TRAFALGAR, HE DIED AT MARLBRO' GRANGE, 23rd
DECEMBER 1867 AGED 82
DEARLY BELOVED

"I KNOW THAT HE SHALL RISE AGAIN"

WILLIAM WYNNE EYTON

William Wynne Eyton was the fourth son of the Reverend Hope Wynne Eyton, of Leeswood, in the county of Flint. He was born at Wrexham in Denbighshire in 1794, and entered the service in 1805 when just 11 years old, serving as a volunteer first class and later as a midshipman on board the *Neptune,* a 98-gun first-rate ship-of-the-line. Young William's baptism of fire was to be the Battle of Trafalgar, and the memory of this action would stay with him all his life.

The *Neptune*, under the command of Thomas Fremantle, was the third ship in the column led by Lord Nelson, and so was very quickly in the thick of the action and hotly engaged. The *Neptune's* losses during the battle were ten men killed and a further 33 wounded, some very badly. To the 11-year-old boy the roar of cannon, the smoke and shot, the buzz of flying splinters of oak and the screams and groans of injured and dying men, must all have seemed far removed from the peace and tranquillity of the family estate of Leeswood Hall, with its fine woodlands and quiet country setting.

William survived Trafalgar unharmed. Later in his naval career he served in many other actions, and only appears to have been wounded once. He served in the *Seahorse* (38) and was present at the capture of the Turkish frigate *Badere Zaffer* (44) in 1808. In 1811 he joined in succession the *Ville de Paris* (110) and *Rodney* (74). In 1813, we find him in the *Milford* (74) at the capture of Fiume and Trieste, and in 1814 he was promoted to lieutenant. He continued in service until June 16th 1832, when he was invalided from the *Asia* (84) on half pay, and was not employed again.

From naval records it seems his last ship was the *Lightning* steamer; he was appointed to her in 1830 for the purpose of conveying Charles X, from Lulworth to Leith. In 1852 further promotion came and he was made up to commander, receiving for his services the war medal with two clasps. It appears he spent his retirement at the family estate, and it was at Leeswood on June 6th 1857 that he died. He was laid to rest in the Leeswood vault in Pont Blyddyn Church, Flintshire, on June 13th 1857. There is a stained glass window in the chancel of the church, featuring Christ in a small sailing vessel with accompanying figures. A brass plaque beneath states:

To the glory of God and to the memory of William Wynne Eyton. R.N. who died June 6th 1857 aged 63. This window was erected by his surviving brothers and sister.

Leeswood Hall (1726) was the family home of the Wynne Eytons up until 1981, when the last family resident, Mrs Violet Hope Wynne Eyton, died and was laid along with William in the Leeswood vault in the quiet Flintshire churchyard near the estate.

An obituary in the *Liverpool Mercury* for Friday June 12th 1857 on page 7 column five, reads:

June 6th, at Leeswood, the seat of his brother, J. Wynne Eyton Esq. Capt. W.W. Eyton who was one of the few survivors among those who were engaged in the memorable Battle of Trafalgar, Oct 21. 1805 on which occasion he served as midshipman in the Neptune.

In fact William Wynne Eyton only reached the rank of commander, not captain as stated in his obituary.

The Leeswood vault in Pont Blyddyn churchyard is surrounded by railings and is in good condition. There is no inscription save the word 'Leeswood'. In the church are numerous memorials to the family.

THOMAS GOBLE

The son of James Holmes Goble, a major in the Sussex Yeomanry Horse Artillery, he was born in Arundel in approximately 1780.

Rated as master's mate in the *Victory*, he served as Captain Hardy's secretary. After John Scott had been killed by a shot that cut him almost in two, Goble succeeded him for a few minutes as Nelson's secretary, since Captain's Clerk Whipple had also been killed.

Thomas Goble appears in Benjamin West's painting of the battle, near the fallen Nelson. He was appointed purser in 1806 and retired in 1825. Goble was one of the last surviving officers of the *Victory* at Trafalgar and received a medal and clasp. He died in 1869 aged 89 and was buried in St Mary's churchyard, Portchester, near Portsmouth. There is an entry in St Mary's burial register stating:

Buried 10th December 1869
Thomas Goble of Fareham, aged 89.

There does not, however, appear to have been any record of a headstone to him.

JOHN GREENLY B.A.

Reverend Greenly was appointed chaplain, Royal Navy in 1804. He served as chaplain aboard the *Revenge* (74) at Trafalgar and was wounded.

After leaving the service he became a minor Canon of Salisbury Cathedral, perpetual Curate of St Thomas, and Rector of Sharncote, Wiltshire. He received the Naval General Service medal and clasp for Trafalgar and died at Salisbury in 1862.

On the north side of the cloisters in Salisbury Cathedral is a mural tablet which reads:

Near this spot, on the green, lie the
remains of the Rev. John Greenly M.A.
50 years Priest Vicar of this Cathedral
and 40 years Vicar of St. Thomas in this
City; who died December 1 1862, Aged
85 yrs. And of Mary his wife, who died
at Laverstock March 15th 1866, aged
88 years. Also four of their Grand-
children who died in this close in the
short space of one month A.D. 1855.

This Tablet was erected by their son,
in Loving Memory 1887

There is also an individual tombstone in the cloister garth which reads:

John Greenly, died December 1st 1862 aged 85

ROBERT & STEPHEN HILTON

Stephen Hilton was born in Kent in 1785 and entered the service in 1795 as a volunteer third class. At Trafalgar he was master's mate of the *Minotaur* (74). He was promoted to lieutenant in 1806, and in the same year took part in the capture of four French frigates off Rochefort whilst serving in the *Revenge* (74). He retired as Commander in 1839, received a Naval General Service Medal with two clasps, and died in 1872.

Stephen's brother Robert served as surgeon's mate on board the *Swiftsure* (74) at Trafalgar, and died in 1837.

Both brothers are buried in the churchyard of St Mary the Virgin, Selling, Kent. On the south side of the churchyard there is a limestone memorial which reads:

> *In memory of Stephen Hilton late commander who died 21st February 1872 in his ......th year. "Precious in the sight of the Lord is the death of his saints".*

There is an entry is in the Burial Register of Selling Church:

> *Stephen Hilton of Trafalgar House, Selling, 25th February 1872 aged 85 years.*

Trafalgar House still stands today in the village. Stephen used his Trafalgar prize money to add the front part to a Tudor cottage previously known as 'Bolly's' .

Hanging in the church of St Mary the Virgin are two flags which were flown at Trafalgar: the Union Jack flown by the *Minotaur*, the other a Spanish ensign flown by the *Neptune*. On the south chancel south-west wall is a round copper plaque which describes the presentation of the flags to the church by the Hilton family.

Robert Hilton was 21 when he wrote the following letter to his youngest brother William, then aged 18. The letter is reproduced by kind permission of Mrs A D M Hilton and Mr Neame.

Dear William,

The proceeding narrative I flatter myself will not be unpleasant to you and family. On Sat the 19th Oct the Commander in Chief made the Signal General to Chase S.E. at half past eleven beat to quarters and cleared ship for action, these preparations naturally led us to imagine the combined Fleets had made their escape from Cadiz, and it is impossible to express the anxiety we felt lest they should once more elude the vigilence of our gallant Admiral. We made all sail to the S.E. 20th at ½ past six a.m. ...... The lookout ships to Leeward continued all night burning blue lights, Sky Baskets, and repeatedly firing guns as signals.

At 5 a.m. the following day to the universal satisfaction of all our British seamen the enemies fleet hove in sight, we with great alacrity made all possible sail in chase, and beat to quarters, we now made sure of our fugitive enemy to the inexpressible pleasure of the whole crew: to our great gratification the enemy hove to and formed the line of Battle in two divisions. At ½ past 12 the Admiral Collingwood commenced the action with a fire of thunder breaking through their line, in the course of half an hour the smoke which surrounded the Royal Sovereigne cleared away and we had the pleasure of seeing several of the enemies ships completely dismantled. We were at this time nearly alongside of the enemys Lee Line which was engaged ....

The first ship which fired into us was a Spanish 3 decker, we did not fire a shot till we came well within gunshot but though we had received their fire very patiently at the first, they had no reason to be dissatisfied with the fire we returned her. Now it was our seamen displayed that nautical skill which rank them superior to every nation in the universe while they navigate the wooden walls that protect old Albion and compel the world to own them favourites of Neptune. The Victory was at this time observed to be in the heat of action with the top of her Mizen Topmast over her side. We stood the enemys line. The Polyphemus cheered us as we passed her which was returned with a spirited Huzza from our people.

We shortly afterwards observed the Defiance alongside a French 80 gun ship named L'Aigle, when a broadside or two from us reduced the Frenchman to the necessity of hauling down her colours to the Defiance. When we first fired into her the Defiance had boarded her and were driving the Frenchmen overboard in all directions, we now passed under the stern of the Bellisle totally dismantled, the Union Jack and St. George's Ensign were still displayed on the stumps of her masts and though an immovable log upon the water they still kept up a smart fire on the enemy whenever it was possible to bring a gun clear of the wreck; this was a scene which accorded well with the feelings of an Englishman. When we came close up with her, the ships companies were crowded on the beams, Poop and quarters and every other part of the ship to cheer us, which they did by giving loud Huzzas which we were not dilatory in returning.

Capt Hargood requested Capt Rutherford would engage a ship to windward which was firing into him as it was impossible for him to return the fire as he could not work his ship. We now came up with the Frenchman who was now running down to us: it was at this time our Ship company displayed real and determined resolution to <u>conquer</u> or <u>die</u>. We maintained so heavy a fire on the ship that we not only cut away her Main and Mizen masts in the course of an hour and half, but set fire to her in various places particularly the Fore Top: she now ceased firing and we were on the point of sending a Cutter (to take possession of her) which we had lowered down, when Prince opened a smart fire on her, and she in a few minutes became enveloped in flames.

The action was by this time decided in a manner (I trust it always will while the enemies of England contend with her for the dominion of the seas) viz:- in the total defeat of the Combind. We observed 4 sail of the line crowding all the sail they possibly could before the wind to escape. We were unable to follow them as most of our standing rigging was cut so much we were under the necessity of laying to to repair our damages, our Gaff, our Mizen and Mizen Topmast much wounded, and our Foremast and Mainmast had received much shot. The Bellisle some time after came alongside of us, taken in tow by the Euralus, we turned the hands up to cheer her as she passed us. Capt Hargood hailed us and told Capt Rutherford he felt himself greatly obliged to our Ship's company for their spirited conduct in protecting the Bellisle from the fire of the Frenchman.

At 7 p.m. sent a Master's mate with a lieutenant and a party of Marines on board the Berwick to assist in securing her and getting her into port, the Berwick being a French prize. At 9 p.m., the prize Master of the Redoubtable hailed us and requested us to give him some assistance as the prize was in a most wretched situation as they were scarcely able to keep the ship above water though they employed all hands (Prisoners not excepted) at the pumps. We immediately sent a hawser on board and took the ship in tow, at the same time sending a lieutenant and party of seamen to assist the Prize master; it was impossible to ascertain yet how many ships had struck to the British flag, the fleets were so much scattered, and it so soon became dark after the action.

On the 22 it came on to blow a most violent gale of wind, but the prize in tow seemed to weather it tolerably well, notwithstanding her shattered state, till about 3 in the afternoon, when from the violence of the rolling in a heavy sea, she carried away the foremast the only mast she had standing: towards evening she made repeated signals of distress to us, we now hoisted out our boats and sent them on board to save if possible the people on board of her, although there was a tremendous sea running and we were fearful lest the boats would be swamped alongside the Prize, but they happily succeeded in bringing off the greater part of them from the wreck as well as our own Lieutenant and part of the seamen we sent on board, with the Lieutenant, and two Midshipmen with some of the seamen all belonging to the Temeraire: if our situation was disagreeable from fatigue and inclemency of the weather, what must not the unfortunate prisoners have suffered on board the Redoubtable, previous to the action she had 800 men, nearly 500 were killed and wounded in action, and many of the surviving 300 perished, what added to the horrors of the night was the inability of saving them all, as we could no longer intrust the lives of our men in the open boats at the mercy of a heavy sea, and most violent gale of wind.

At 10 p.m. the Redoubtable went down, and the hawser by which we still kept her in tow (in order if the weather moderated and the prize be able to weather the night through, we might once more endeavour to save the remainder of her crew) was carried away with the violence of the shock, this was now the most dreadful scene I have ever witnessed we could distinctly hear the cries of the unhappy people we could no longer assist.

Towards the morning the weather moderated, and we had the good fortune to save many that were floating passed us on pieces of wreck; at 9 of the 23rd we discovered a large raft ahead, and shortly afterwards a second, many of the unfortunate people were seen clinging to the wreck, the merciless sea threatening almost instant destruction to them, the boats were immediately lowered down and we happily saved 36 people from the fury of the waves. When the boats came alongside many of these unfortunate men were unable to get up the ship's sides, as most of them were not only fainting from fatigue but were wounded in a most shocking manner, some expired in the boats before they could be brought alongside completely exhausted and worn out with struggleing to reserve their lives the whole of the tempestuous night upon a few crazy planks exposed to over inclemency of weather. If our seamen had conducted themselves as brave men during the action, now it was they showed themselves as humane and generous as they were brave, when these unfortuneate prisoners came on board, you might have seen them clothing them as well as a seaman's scanty stock would permit of, though scanty yet hard earnt, and in defence of the King, his family and his country at large.

About 11 we discovered the remaining part of the combined Fleets, we now made every preparation for the renewal of the Action, shortly after we hailed the Victory to inquire for the health of Lord Nelson who we had heard was wounded at the commencement of the Action, when we received the melancholy information from Capt Hardy that this hero was no more, his dying words were, after being informed that 19 sail of the line had struck, he the warlike Admiral made answer "I have lived then long enough".

This unwelcome intelligence troubled us most sensibly, those hearts that a moment previous elated with the success that had crowned our Navy, and our gallant seamen now paused a while to pay the tribute due to the memory of so great a character, though he is not again to be the brave Admiral that has repeatedly led the British to victory and struck the hearts of the enemy with terror, nor again to be a friend to the distressed seamen, and the protector of the indigent widows and orphans, yet will the memory of so great a Hero be for ever respected while England has a name, and when posterity recounts the actions of this veteran in her service, it will justly own him the glory in defence of his country: and his last telegraphic signal was "England this day expects every man will do his duty"....

Robert Hilton

EDWARD JONES

Born in Leicester in 1777, this officer was appointed second lieutenant 115 Company, Plymouth on May 26th 1795. He was then promoted to first lieutenant Company 134, Plymouth on November 28th 1796. His grand-daughter, Victoria, stated in a short history of her grandfather's career that he was serving in the *Penelope* (38) at the capture of the *Guillaume Tell* (80) and in Egypt was ADC to General Doyle. For his services he received the Sultan's medal, which is shown in his portrait which now hangs in Leicester Museum and Art Gallery, together with his wife's portrait which was painted in 1815/20.

His wife was born in 1791 at Gainsborough, Lincolnshire and for some time Major Jones lived in Infirmary Square, Leicester. He was lieutenant in the frigate *Naiad* (38) at Trafalgar, although his promotion was granted on August 15th 1805 to captain of the 37th Company, Chatham.

Captain Jones then appears to have retired from the active list of the Marines in 1810, to become Brevet Major in 1819, and he finally retired in 1826.

Major Edward Jones died in 1866 and was buried in Welford Road Cemetery, Leicester on March 15th in section A 1 (consecrated) No 134. Also interred are his wife, two other members of his family, and his grand-daughter Victoria Jones who joined her grandfather on April 12th 1945, at the age of 82.

Major Jones had two sons who also served in the Marines, Captain Ebenezer Tristram Jones and Captain James Jones.

WILLIAM KELLY

Appointed lieutenant to the *Haarlem* (64) in 1799, William Kelly then became, in 1804, lieutenant in the *Illustrious* (74), in which he remained till 1810.

In 1805, whilst Nelson pursued Villeneuve to the West Indies, the Admiralty ordered Collingwood to blockade Cadiz and Cartagena. One of the ships in the blockade was the *Illustrious*.

Off Cape Finisterre, on May 27th 1805, Collingwood was informed by Sir Richard Bickerton, in the *Queen* (98), that Nelson was after the combined fleet. Collingwood immediately sent his two fastest ships *Ramilies* (74) and *Illustrious* to catch up and reinforce his old friend. On July 2nd 1805, in a letter to the Reverend Dr Carlyle, Collingwood writes:

> *I sent two ships to strengthen my friend*
> *in the West Indies, and the rest are*
> *divided between the two ports here.*

Kelly was promoted to commander whilst serving as first lieutenant of the *Illustrious*, under Captain Broughton, on October 21st 1810. In 1814 he commanded the brig *Insolent* (14) which was sent on a recruiting expedition to the Isle of Man in that year. Impressment had been a serious problem for the Manx men during the wars against France. The island had a population of less than 28,000 and its existence depended upon its fishermen. Too easily these fell to the press-gang, and it is sobering to think that the island did not have a port that could even boast of a square-rigged vessel at this time. Indeed Lord Teignmouth, who visited the island wrote in 1829:

> *The Isle of Man has perhaps furnished a*
> *much larger number of able and excellent*
> *seamen to the public service, in proportion*
> *to its population, than any other*
> *individual district of the British Empire.*

In 1817 Captain Kelly retired to his home parish of Ballaugh, Isle of Man, where he owned part of the Ravensdale estate in Ballaugh Glen and built the first house there. His house, now the Ravensdale Castle Hotel, is situated in the charming Glen Dhoo alongside a sparkling trout stream.

Captain Kelly died in 1823 and lies buried in the old churchyard of St Mary de Ballaugh. His grave is surrounded by iron railings and a flat stone bears the simple inscription:

In Memory of
WILLIAM KELLY R.N.
who departed this life
Nov. the 17th 1823
aged 52

At the turn of the century the commissions to Captain Kelly's ships were in the possession of Mr G Preston, grandson of Captain Kelly's housekeeper, Eleanor Kewish. A silver cup together with his cocked hat were given to Mrs Kewish and later passed on to her eldest son Thomas Corlett of Liverpool. Mr Preston's sister had Captain Kelly's gold snuff box.

WILLIAM LAUGHARNE

The son of Captain Thomas Laugharne and nephew of Vice-Admiral of the White, John Laugharne, William was born at Poole, Dorset on December 21st 1785. He entered the Navy in January 1898 as a midshipman aboard the *Barfleur* (98) under Captain J R Dacres.

William Laugharne was one of Nelson's 'young gentlemen' on board the *Foudroyant (80).* He witnessed the surrender of Naples in June 1799 and the subsequent capture of the *Genereux* (74) the *Ville de Marseilles* (a store ship), and the *Guillaume Tell* (80). This must have given Nelson great satisfaction as they were the only French ships to have escaped the Battle of the Nile the previous year.

William Laugharne then followed Sir Edward Berry into the *Princess Charlotte* (36) and *Ruby* (64) until the peace of Amiens. At the renewal of hostilities he served aboard the *Concorde* (36) and *Tremendous* (74) and was then appointed by Sir Edward Pellew to act as lieutenant of the frigate *Cornwallis* (44) on the East India station. His first commission is dated November 14th 1806. He served as his uncle's flag-lieutenant at Malta where he received his final rank of commander on September 23rd 1814.

Captain Laugharne married twice. His only brother, Thomas, was lost in the brig *Jaseur* (12) when crossing the Bay of Bengal in August 1809.

William Laugharne died in 1856 and is buried in the churchyard of St Martin's, Laugharne, Carmarthen. His inscription reads:

SACRED
TO THE MEMORY OF
CAPTAIN
WILLIAM LAUGHARNE
ROYAL NAVY
WHO DIED
IN THE CITY OF BATH
NOVEMBER 6th 1856
Aged 71 years.

OF HIM IT MAY BE JUSTLY RECORDED THAT
TO HIS COUNTRY, HIS RELATIVES, HIS FRIENDS
AND THE POOR OF THIS PARISH HE FAITHFULLY
DID HIS DUTY IN THAT STATE OF LIFE TO WHICH
IT HAS PLEASED GOD TO CALL HIM.

Also in the Church of St Martin's are wall plaques to Admiral John Laugharne and a dedication to him by William, whose will is inscribed in marble alongside.

A silver salver, which the church displays at Easter and Christmas, was once the possession of Thomas Laugharne, William's great-uncle. It bears the inscription:

> *The Gift of the Honourable The Dutch East*
> *India Co. to Thomas Laugharne Esqr. Com. of his*
> *Majesty's Sloop of War the Scout in memory of*
> *his faithful assistance to the Dutch East India*
> *Company's ship "Barbesteyn" Capn. Van Vlaanderen,*
> *when the crew mutinied in the Downs on 29th November 1786.*

The salver also states:

> *Bequeathed to the Vicar and Churchwardens of the*
> *Parish of Laugharne for the use of the Communion*
> *Table of the Parish Church by Captain William*
> *Laugharne, Royal Navy, who died in the City of Bath*
> *on 6th November 1856.*

Two smaller salvers and a large flagon were given by the wife of Lord Cornwallis to the church. On the south wall is a large oil painting by Benjamin West, who painted the 'Death of Wolfe' and later the 'Death of Nelson'. It shows the prophet Jeremiah with an almond branch.

This 13th-century church has a great deal of interest to offer, and the visitor will find in the new part of the churchyard the burial place of the poet Dylan Thomas, who lived in Laugharne for some years and whose boat-house and writing shed are open to view.

A replica of the poets' plaque in Westminster Abbey is on the north wall of the church next to Captain William Laugharne's.

Also commemorated with a plaque is Major Thomas Rees of the Royal Marines, who died on January 27th 1857, aged 74.

Another item of naval interest is an entry in the parish records, dated April 3rd 1795, which reads:

> *Pursuant to the notice duly given for the purpose of raising two land men for His Majesty's Navy - additional rates be made to the poor rate towards a bounty to be given to these two.*

DAVID LEWIS

David Lewis was one of the two people of the same name who served on board the *Conqueror* (74) at Trafalgar, who received a Naval General Service medal with clasp. He was either an ordinary seaman or able bodied.

Very little is known of him, other than that he lived at High Street, Aberystwyth, Wales and had a wife called Mary. What is certain is that his ship the *Conqueror*, captained by Israel Pellew, was in the thick of the action at Trafalgar, being the fourth ship in the weather column. The French Commander-in-Chief, Villeneuve, aboard the *Bucentaure* (74), surrendered his sword to Captain Atcherley, Royal Marines, of the *Conqueror*.

During the battle, the *Conqueror's* figure head was shot away, and the crew asked permission for it to be replaced by a likeness of Nelson. This was granted, and when the ship finally docked at Plymouth, the work was completed and ornamented at the crew's own expense.

David Lewis died in 1850 aged 66 and was buried in St Michael's churchyard, Aberystwyth, alongside the remains of the old castle. The churchyard has now been cleared and made into an ornamental park. The original slate stones are banked around lawns and flower borders to good effect.

David Lewis's stone stands against the wall of the old vestry, nearer the castle than the present church. The inscription reads:

STOP, TRAVELLER, STOP AND READ

This stone was erected by those
who fully Appreciated the integrity,
and fidelity of DAVID LEWIS,
alias (the old Commodore) who
departed this life on the
16th day of Feb^{ry} 1850.
AGED 66 YEARS.
He nobly fought on board the "Conqueror" 74
Under NELSON at the battle of Trafalgar
and for the last 13 years perform'd
Zealously the duties of deputy
Harbour Master at this Port.
Here lies David Lewis? what then
David - when his Master calls will rise again.

WILLIAM NICHOLSON

William Nicholson is buried in the churchyard of St Mary the Virgin, Wendens Ambo, Essex, near the south porch.

The inscription on the flat gravestone has been badly eroded, but was fortunately recorded by John J Mackay in his book *Wendens Ambo - the history of an Essex village:*

> *In loving memory of William Nicholson*
> *of this parish. Midshipman in Nelson's*
> *Vanguard who died December 16th 1886*
> *in his 104th year.*
> *"At evening time it shall be light"*

From the burial register it appears that the funeral took place on December 18th 1886, conducted by the vicar of Newport, G F Tamplin. Against the entry in the register the vicar had written: 'query whether his age was as much by several years'. The cause of death was given as old age. However, the vicar's suspicions were not borne out, as census returns for 1861 and 1871 state him to be a widower, retired from business aged 77, born at Fareham, Hampshire. In the 1871 census he appears as an annuitant (pensioner).

With regard to his naval career, he was promoted lieutenant on February 14th 1803. He served in the *Seine* (36) in 1804, and the *San Antonio* (74) in 1814. It is likely that he was present at the Battle of the Nile in 1798. He disappeared from the Navy list in 1815.

He moved into 'Rose Cottage' owned by Mr Robinson in about 1850, and became one of the best remembered Victorians of the village, solely because of the inscription on his monument.

JOHN OLIVER

Richard Whitting Egan, in his book *Liverpool Colonnade* writes about the old cemetery behind the Anglican Cathedral and gives a clue to the final resting place of a Nelson Hero, named John Oliver. He writes:

All about you are the graves of sailors and master mariners, among them lies Captain John Oliver, veteran of the battles of the Nile, Copenhagen and Trafalgar in which he served under Lord Nelson on HMS Victory. He died in 1876 at the advanced age of 102.

A search of the graveyard soon reveals that the gravestone written about by Mr Egan, has been removed. However the records for St James' Cemetery have all been kept and are now in Picton Library, Liverpool. The burial register states:

No/40435. John Oliver - Northumberland St 2nd April aged 102. Minister Mr Bannister.'

The monumental inscription book also gives information about Oliver's grave, it states:

Captain John Oliver
Fought on HMS Victory under Lord Nelson
Also a veteran of the Battles of the Nile,
Copenhagen, and Trafalgar.
Died 27.3.1876 aged 102
Also Jane Oliver Died 8.12.1847. aged 61
Also John Owen Oliver Died 8.12.1903, aged 63

Although, sadly, the memorial stone is gone, the exact site of John's grave has been located with the help of cemetery plans.

The *Liverpool Mercury* for Wednesday March 29th 1876 gives the following obituary:

Oliver, March 27th, at his son's residence 94 Northumberland Street aged 102 Captain John Oliver. Will be interred on Sunday morning April 2nd at 9 a.m. at St James Cemetery.

The next day, March 30th, the *Mercury* gives the following report:

Death of a Trafalgar Hero in Liverpool.

The fine old veterans of the Napoleonic wars, living links between the present and the memorable past, are too rapidly passing away from us. Captain John Oliver, a centenarian, who as stated in our obituary of yesterday, died in Liverpool on Monday, was one of those interesting men. At the time of his death he had reached the great age of 102 years 2 months, and a few days, having been born on the 18th January 1774. He was a native of Devonshire, here the earlier years of his boyhood were spent. Conceiving a liking for the sea, he ran away from his home, near Tavistock, at the age of ten, and went to North Shields, whence he sailed on his first voyage. Soon after the close of his apprenticeship, in 1793, he fell a prey to the pressgang, and became a man-of-wars man.

In 1798 he was serving on board the Bellerophon, and was present at the battle of the Nile. Though his ship suffered terribly, he came out of the engagement unhurt, and was afterwards transferred to the Glatton, in which he fought at Copenhagen. After a short period of service on board the Resolution, he was paid off and returned to the mercantile marine. In 1803, however, he again fell into the hands of the pressgang, and was put on board the Victory, in which he served at the battle of Trafalgar.

In 1806 he again returned to the merchant service, in which he remained until he retired from the sea altogether at the age of 86. He generally sailed from Liverpool, and was in the service of Mr Gladstone, father of the ex-premier, Messrs Hurry and Gibson, Messrs Cannon and Miller, and Messrs Wilson, Brown, and Co. Several ships belonging to the last two mentioned firms he commanded. On leaving the sea he found himself without a

110

competence, and for the rest of his life he was supported almost entirely by his pensions and one or two allowances, including one of £12 a year from the Mercantile Marine Association and a small yearly sum from the late Robertson Gladstone. He retained the use of all faculties almost to the last; and having a touch of the garrulity of the old salt, nothing pleased him in his later years so much as to recount the more striking adventures of his remarkable career. He always looked back with pride to his services in the Royal Navy, and was especially proud that he was present at Trafalgar, was one of the crew who received the historic order, and was near the great commander when he died.

There are many recorded facts about John Oliver, however one fact we are unable to verify is whether John was, as he said, on board *Victory* at Trafalgar; his name does not appear on the muster book or any of the ships' records for that time. Could it be that Captain Oliver, with the 'garrulity of the old salt' embellished his naval career? We would like to think not.

EDWARD THORNBOROUGH PARKER

This young officer came to Nelson's attention in the Baltic and soon became a favourite. He accompanied him everywhere as aide-de-camp, from fishing trips, to service off the French coast. It was on a raid at Boulogne, which Nelson thought would be used as a departure point for invasion by the French, that events went badly wrong.

Parker led one of the four divisions in a night attack on August 15th 1801, with Nelson in the *Medusa (32)*. The small boats, however, lost contact with each other and the French were well prepared, repelling boarders with bayonets and grape-shot.

The attack was a failure, similar to the one at Teneriffe, with 44 killed and 126 wounded in the boats. Parker's thigh was shattered, and Nelson put him up in rooms in Deal to recover, but Parker's condition slowly worsened. Lady Hamilton and Sarah Nelson, wife of brother William, visited regularly. In an attempt to stem the gangrene which had set in, his leg was amputated and buried in the grave of midshipmen Gore and Bristow, who had perished in the attack. On September 27th Parker finally died, aged 23. In a letter to Emma Hamilton, Nelson wrote, 'My heart is almost broke and I see I have wrote nonsense, I know not what I am doing.'

Parker's funeral was held next day. The procession was led by 200 men of the Derbyshire Regiment, and his coffin carried by six captains, followed by Nelson who wept openly at the graveside. The *Naval Chronicle* wrote:

Why does the voice of public sorrow swell
Why pours the gallant breast that manly sigh
Why does the tear of gen'rous anguish dwell
On Nelson's cheek and dim his ardent eye?

One simple word the mighty grief will speak,
'Tis PARKER'S death that breathes the gen'ral gloom
That strikes the living glow from Beauty's cheek,
The flow'r of valour wither'd in its bloom.

Parker lies buried in the churchyard of St George's, Deal. His stone, which still stands in the Garden of Rest to the rear of the church, reads:

THIS IS THE TOMB OF CAPTAIN EDWARD THORNBOROUGH PARKER A GALLANT AND DISTINGUISHED COMMANDER WHO, WOUNDED IN ACTION OFF BOULOGNE, DIED ON 27 SEPTEMBER 1801, AGED 23 YEARS. ADMIRAL LORD NELSON WHOSE CLOSE FRIEND HE WAS, ATTENDED HIS FUNERAL

GEORGE SAMUEL PARSONS

St James' Cemetery, Liverpool features again as the final resting place of another of Nelson's Heroes, for here lie the mortal remains of Lieutenant George Parsons. The *Liverpool Mercury* for January 24th 1854 gives the following short obituary:

> *20th January at his residence, Holt Hill, Cheshire, aged 71 years. George Samuel Parsons Esq., Commander RN.*

St James' Cemetery records also give mention to Lieutenant Parsons:

> *Cemetery Records, No./20543. George Samuel Parsons, Holt Hill, Tranmere. Interred, St James' Cemetery 25th January 1854 Aged 71 years.*

A search of the cemetery grounds using a copy of the burial plan soon revealed the site of the grave but sadly the stone had been removed by the local authorities, to make maintenance easier. However, although the stone was gone, we know what the inscription was, thanks to Mr Gibson, who recorded many of the more interesting memorial stones in Liverpool churchyards in the period around 1880. In volume six, page 487, of Gibson's works we find:

Family Grave
of
G.S.Parsons R.N.
and
Catherine his Wife
In memory of
Mary and Anna Westenra
Daughters of the above, at the early age of
9 months
also the above
George Samuel Parsons
Commander R.N. who died January
20th 1854 aged 71 years
also
Charlotte, third daughter of

the above, who died Oct 6 1860
aged 34 years
also the above Catherine Parsons
who died Feb 16 1869 aged 72 years
also George, third son of the above
George Samuel and Catherine Parsons
who died in China in 1836 aged 17 years
also Edward the fifth son
who died at Bombay in 1850 aged 27 years
also Kenyon the sixth son
who died at Calcutta in 1845 aged 18 years

It would appear from this inscription that Parsons was a commander in the Royal Navy. We know, however, that he only reached the rank of lieutenant. One other mistake on the gravestone is the date of death of George, the third son: the inscription states that he died in China in 1836, aged 17 years. His obituary in the *Liverpool Courier* for the 25th October 1837 gives his age as 18 years:

On the coast of China on board the brig 'Fairy' belonging to Messrs Jardine, Matheson and Co, of Canton, George the third son of G S Parsons RN of this town, aged 18 years, whose death was occasioned by mutiny taking place on board that vessel in which Captain M'Kay and all the Europeans were murdered by the Manillamen, who were part of her crew, two of whom are now in custody at Manilla and have confessed to these attrocities.

Lieutenant Parsons first entered the navy in July 1795 as a first class volunteer. He first served on board the *Barfleur* (98) under Captain J R Dacres, with whom he fought as midshipman in the action off Cape St Vincent on February 14th 1797. He moved in April 1798 to the *Foudroyant* (80 guns) where he acted as signal midshipman under Lord Nelson. It was at this time in his career that the young Parsons got to know Emma, Lady Hamilton, and the impression she made upon him would stay with him all his life. George Parsons served in many actions in and around the Mediterranean, and in 1801 on August 6th he was nominated for the post of acting lieutenant and confirmed in this rank on March 25th 1802. For his services in

Egypt, Parsons was presented with a gold medal by the Turkish Government. His naval service continued until 1810, when the state of his health obliged him to go on half-pay, and he was not officially employed again until 1841 when he was commissioned as Admiralty Agent on board a contract mail vessel. During this time he was once wrecked, and was lucky to survive.

Parsons had settled in Liverpool in or around 1810/11 and in 1812 he married a local girl, Catherine Giball, by whom he had eight children. The family stayed on and worked in Liverpool, although they moved house about four times. In 1850 they moved across the river to Tranmere, to take up residence in one of the new villas built on Holt Hill overlooking the Mersey. During his time in Liverpool, when living at 52, Seel Street, (the house is still standing) George Parsons had a book printed called, *Nelsonian Reminiscences: Leaves from Memory's Log.* In this book he recalled his naval service and his time with Lord Nelson and Lady Hamilton, both of whom he held in very high regard. Parsons' work had originally been written for the *Metropolitan Magazine* and it appeared in the course of 1837, 1838, 1839 and 1840. It was first published in book form in Boston, USA and later in 1843, in England. It has gone through many editions and was reprinted as late as 1973. In the *Liverpool Mercury's* literary review, of September 1843, Parsons' work was criticised for its defence of Lord Nelson's conduct in the Mediterranean and also for its mention and regard for Lady Hamilton. Parsons' reply to the editor of the paper was as follows:

*GENTLEMEN, - I am this morning favoured with a copy of the kind and able critique on my humble effort in literature, which you inform me is to appear in tomorrow's paper. I not only most freely accord my consent, but heartily thank you for the honour done me. The late unfortunate Neapolitan admiral, Prince Caraccioli, was doomed to death by his own countrymen, officers of high rank and station, Lord Nelson, as Viceroy, **alone** sanctioned the sentence. The she-wolf, as you are pleased to term her, I depict as I knew her in the palmy days of her beauty and her might, when her smiles were eagerly courted by heroes, and grave sedate statesmen not only respectfully listened to her advice, but adopted her talented, strong, and energetic measures - when her favour was the highroad to promotion, and her*

116

masculine mind governed kingdoms. It would ill become me, Gentlemen, to lend an ear to the scandal that has blackened her fame, and clean blotted from memory her **great services.** *Thus are our virtues written in water, our vices engraven on brass. Not to trespass further on your paper at this late hour, I shall conclude by stating, that when I knew this unfortunate lady, she was the observed of all observers, the honoured and idolized wife of Sir William Hamilton, Bart., not only one of the most learned men of his day, but universally beloved as great and good. - Yours, &c.*

G.S. PARSONS.

*N.B. - Not mentioning Lady Hamilton in Nelsonian reminiscences (***as recommended by you***) would, it strikes me, be on the same principle as omitting the character of Hamlet in the tragedy of that name.*

CHARLES PATRIARCHE

At the Battle of the Nile, Charles Patriarche was master's mate aboard the *Defence* (74) under Captain John Peyton. In May of 1798 she was sent to join Nelson in the Mediterranean, where on the evening of August 1st the British Fleet finally discovered the French Fleet, in Aboukir Bay at the mouth of the Nile. During the battle, the *Defence* was eighth in the line and lost her topmast, although from a crew of 584, only 15 were killed and wounded.

The ship's crew had been involved in the Spithead Mutiny the previous year, and once again got into trouble. One can only wonder at the thoughts of Master's Mate Patriarche when, six weeks after the glorious Nile victory, nineteen of his crew were sentenced to death and six to flogging - more than their losses from the battle.

Promoted to lieutenant and now serving on the *Superb* (74) Charles Patriarche was present at the action in the Gut of Gibraltar, on July 12th 1801, in which the Spanish ships, *Real Carlos* and *San Hermenegildo,* (both 112 guns), and the French *St Antoine* (74), were destroyed.

By the time of his death in 1850 Patriarche had reached captain's rank, and had been awarded the Naval General Service medal with two clasps.   He is buried in the parish churchyard, Hempstead, Gloucester, and his inscription reads:

Sacred to the memory of
CAPTAIN CHARLES PATRIARCHE R.N.
who departed this life
on the 16th day of January 1850
57 years of which had been spent
in the service of his country

His end has peace.

WALTER WILTSHIRE PIKE

The son of Thomas and Sarah Pike, Walter Pike was born in Silver Street, Tetbury, Gloucester, on March 11th 1785.

Walter Pike entered the Navy on July 4th 1798 as an AB on board the *Achille* (74), in which ship he was employed mainly in the Channel. He was then transferred in April 1802, to the *Endymion* (40), under Captain P Durham, lying at Portsmouth. After serving for two years as master's mate in the *Isis* (50), flag-ship of Vice-Admiral James Gambier at Newfoundland, he joined during 1804 the *Royal William* (84), *Swiftsure* (74), and *Glory* (98). Whilst in the *Glory* he became lieutenant on February 20th 1805.

From the sloop *Wolverene* (18) he joined the frigate *Euryalus* (36), under Captain Hon Henry Blackwood, in which he served at Trafalgar. The *Euryalus* was launched in 1803 and on September 15th 1805 in company with the *Victory,* she sailed from Spithead to join the blockading fleet off Cadiz. For the next three weeks in company with the other frigates, the *Euryalus* watched Cadiz harbour and provided invaluable service day and night, being the first link in a chain of communication with Nelson and the main fleet.

On the morning of the battle, Nelson summoned Blackwood on board the *Victory,* and thanked him personally for everything the *Euryalus* had done. Together with Hardy, Blackwood signed as witness to the codicil of Nelson's will, asking for Emma Hamilton to be cared for, in the event of his death, by his country. At Trafalgar the *Euryalus* was to windward of the weather column, and was used by Collingwood to relay signals. Although not actually engaged, she had her main and top mast rigging shot away. After the battle, Collingwood shifted his flag to the *Euryalus* which in turn towed the *Royal Sovereign* (100) to safety.

Walter Pike then became first Lieutenant of the *Mermaid* (32) in 1809, and of the *Achates* (16 guns).   Under Captain Morrison of the *Achates*, Pike was involved in a running action of several hours with the French frigate *La Trave* (44), off the coast of France. The French frigate was finally captured two days later by the *Andromache* (38), under Captain Tobin.

The *Achates* was paid off in November 1815, and Walter Pike, who did not go to sea again accepted the rank of commander, on August 12th 1840.   He died in 1849, and was buried in the church at Tetbury, Gloucester.   There is a memorial slab on the south side of the east wall in the church which reads:

To the memory of
WALTER WILTSHIRE PIKE
Commander Royal Navy
Son of the late
Thomas and Sarah Pike
of this Parish.
He died at Bristol, Dec. 7th 1849
Aged 64
And his remains lie interred
within this church.

Capt. Pike served as Lieutenant
in the "EURYALUS" frigate
at the ever memorable battle of
TRAFALGAR
and was not less respected in his
profession as an officer
than he was esteemed by a large
circle of friends
in private life as a gentleman.

SETH PUDSEY

George Pudsey BA, Rector of Kirby Underdale, Yorkshire, who died in 1772, had two sons, George and Seth, and had acquired property in the parish. The marriage of Seth Pudsey took place on February 16th 1787. He was a Yeoman farmer living at Manor House Farm, Uncleby, Yorkshire. His son George also lived at Manor House Farm until 1859 when he sold it to Sir Charles Wood, 1st Lord Halifax.

What little of Seth Pudsey's Naval career is known, is mentioned in an obituary in the *Liverpool Mercury & Courier* dated January 16th 1846, page 35 and January 14th 1846 page 7.

At Uncleby near Pocklington Yorks, aged 87 Mr. Seth Pudsey. He served under Ad'l Lord Nelson in various engagements, in one of which he received a bullet in his right shoulder which passed through his body near his heart and was taken from his left side, after which he lived nearly fifty years. The bullet is now in the possession of the deceased's family. He was for sixty years a consistent member of the Wesleyan Methodist Society.

He is buried in Kirby Underdale churchyard, Yorkshire on the south-east side of the church. The inscription on his headstone reads:

Sacred to the memory of
Seth Pudsey of Uncleby,
who died Dec. 29th 1845
Aged 86 years.
also
Hannah Pudsey, wife of the above
who died Aug. 7th 1842
Aged 86 years
The memory of the just is Blessed.

Entry in burial register, Kirby Underdale:

Seth Pudsey of Uncleby   Buried Jan. 2nd 1846   Aged 87
H.D. Erskine (Rector)

JOHN QUILLIAM

John Quilliam was born in Ballakelly, Morown, Isle of Man in 1771 and baptised at the old parish church of Kirk Morown on September 29th 1771. Ironically, in view of Quilliam's future career, Morown is the only parish in the island which does not touch the sea.

He was the eldest son of farmer John Quilliam and Christian Clucas. He began his working life apprenticed to a stone mason, and was then apparently pressed into the Navy whilst fishing in Castletown Bay.

In September of 1791 he is recorded aboard the *Lion* (64) as a supernumerary, for victuals only and not as official crew, but in May 1792 he enlisted and spent two and a half years on this ship, mainly in Chinese waters.

At the battle of Camperdown in 1797 he was acting lieutenant in *Triumph* (74) and was promoted lieutenant by 1798. On October 17th 1799 he was third lieutenant of the *Ethalion* (38) frigate, under Captain Young. Whilst serving on this ship he received £5000 prize money from the capture of the treasure ship *Thetis*. This made Quilliam quite comfortably off, and in 1807 he bought two farms, Ballacallin Moar and Ballacallin Beg. The larger, in the parish of Morown, he named 'Merton', no doubt with his late chief in mind.

At the battle of Copenhagen in 1801, as lieutenant aboard the *Amazon* (38) he first attracted the attention of Nelson, having taken command when all senior to him had been killed. After a brief spell at home he was appointed as lieutenant of the *Victory* and served in her at Trafalgar. During the battle, together with the Master Atkinson, he supervised the steering of the ship using a block and tackle system, as the wheel had been shot away.

After the battle he was given the command of the *Aetna*. In December 1805 he was made post captain and in February 1806 was given command of the prize *San Ildefonso* (74).

Between 1806 and 1808 Quilliam resided in the Isle of Man and was elected to the House of Keys in 1807. He did not resign his membership until 1810, although he was back at sea in 1808 commanding the *Spencer* (74).

In 1812 Captain Quilliam commanded the *Crescent* (38), which took him to the Western Atlantic where he captured an American privateer. Before his retirement in 1815 he also captained the *Alexandria* (32) and the *Inconstant* (36). In 1817 he re-entered the House of Keys and took a particular interest in the fishing industry.

On December 21st 1817 he married Margaret Stevenson whose family owned the estate of Balladoole, Kirk Arbory. The wedding took place by special dispensation, in the conservatory of her house Ballakeigan, and was conducted by the Reverend J Brown. After the marriage they lived at Ballakeigan and spent the winters in a house at Castletown, opposite Castle Rushen. Both houses still exist, Ballakeigan being a particularly fine detached house just outside Castletown.

Captain Quilliam died on October 10th 1829 aged 59 at the 'White House', Kirk Michael. The home of his friend Colonel Goldie, this detached Georgian house is also still standing. Quilliam was buried at Arbory churchyard in the Stevenson vault of his wife's family. There is a very fine stained glass window in the church, with a landscape view, a memorial to the Stevenson family.

On the wall of the church is a memorial to Quilliam from his wife which reads:

SACRED TO THE MEMORY OF
JOHN QUILLIAM ESQR CAPN IN THE ROYAL NAVY
IN HIS EARLY SERVICE HE WAS APPOINTED BY ADML
LORD DUNCAN TO ACT AS LIEUTENANT AT THE BATTLE
OF CAMPERDOWN, AFTER THE VICTORY WAS ACHIEVED,
THIS APPOINTMENT WAS CONFIRMED, HIS GALLANTRY
AND PROFESSIONAL SKILL AT THE BATTLE OF
COPENHAGEN ATTRACTED THE NOTICE OF LORD
NELSON, WHO SUBSEQUENTLY SOUGHT FOR HIS
SERVICES ON BOARD HIS OWN SHIP, AND AS HIS
LORDSHIPS FIRST LIEUT. HE STEERED THE VICTORY
INTO ACTION AT THE BATTLE OF TRAFALGAR, BY THE
EXAMPLE OF DUNCAN AND NELSON HE LEARNED TO
CONQUER; BY HIS OWN MERIT HE ROSE TO COMMAND.
ABOVE ALL THIS HE WAS AN HONEST MAN, THE
NOBLEST WORK OF GOD. AFTER MANY YEARS OF
HONOURABLE AND DISTINGUISHED PROFESSIONAL
SERVICE HE RETIRED TO THIS THE LAND OF HIS
AFFECTIONATE SOLICITUDE AND BIRTH, WHERE IN HIS
PUBLIC STATION AS A MEMBER OF THE HOUSE OF KEYS,
AND IN PRIVATE LIFE HE WAS IN ARDUOUS TIMES THE
UNCOMPROMISING DEFENDER OF THE RIGHTS AND
PRIVILEGES OF HIS COUNTRYMEN, AND THE ZEALOUS
AND ABLE SUPPORTER OF EVERY MEASURE TENDING TO
PROMOTE THE WELFARE AND THE BEST INTERESTS OF
HIS COUNTRY. HE DEPARTED THIS LIFE ON THE 10th
OCTOBER 1829 IN THE 59th YEAR OF HIS AGE. THIS
MONUMENT IS ERECTED BY MARGT C. QUILLIAM TO THE
MEMORY OF HER BELOVED HUSBAND.

The Manx Museum in Douglas has on display Captain Quilliam's uniform together with his commission to the *Crescent* in 1810, his sword, telescope, pocket compass, watch and a box of four decanters. The uniform was last worn in 1823 at a ball given by the Duke of Athol.

In 1941 a descendant of Captain Quilliam, Surgeon General H W Stevenson, apparently had in his possession an oil painting of the Captain, together with miniatures of him and his wife, and correspondence to the Captain.

LEWIS BUCKLE REEVES

Lewis Buckle Reeves was the son of Thomas Reeves and Ellen, daughter of Lewis Buckle, of Borden, East Meon, Hampshire, and the grandson of Robert Reeves of Besborough, Killiner, County Clare, Ireland. Reeves became second lieutenant Royal Marines in 1804. He served at this rank in the *Victory* at Trafalgar, where he was badly wounded. He can be seen in the background of Benjamin West's painting of the Death of Nelson, being assisted by fellow marines.

He was present at the defeat of the French at Babagné near St Louis in 1809, having become first lieutenant in 1807. Retiring on half pay in 1817, Reeves moved to the Isle of Man where he married Anne Jane Scott at Braddan, on July 27th 1821.

Between 1822 and 1833 they had daughters Louisa Scott, Eliza Eleanor, Louisa Anne and Laura Buckle Moore. A son L B Reeves died in 1835 aged two. They lived for a number of years at Stanley Terrace and the Villa Bella Vista, Douglas. Lieutenant Lewis Buckle Reeves died on May 3rd 1861 aged 75 years, and was buried in Onchan churchyard, where Captain Bligh was married many years previously.

Lieutenant Reeves is buried near the top road entrance, next to a chap called Nelson, and has a table top tomb which reads:

> *LIEUT^T· LEWIS BUCKLE REEVES*
> *ROYAL MARINES*
> *SON OF THE LATE THOMAS REEVES M.D.*
> *OF CORK: IRELAND*
> *AND ELEANOR, NEE BUCKLE HIS WIFE*
> *DIED 3rd MAY 1861*
> *AGED 75 YEARS*
> *HE WAS THE LAST SURVIVING OFFICER*
> *WHO FOUGHT ON BOARD THE FLAGSHIP*
> *VICTORY AT TRAFALGAR.*

In his will he left £1200 to his daughters and a copy of the painting 'Death of Nelson' and a silver medal from the Queen for Trafalgar to Louisa Anne Whiteside, née Reeves.

The Manx paper *Monas Herald* ran an obituary in May 1861 which read:

On Friday, the 3rd instant, at the residence of his son-in-law, 8 Prospect Hill, Douglas, LEWIS BUCKLE REEVES, Esquire, Lieutenant of the Royal Marines, aged 75. The deceased, in 1805, then only 19 years of age, served as second Lieutenant on board the Victory at the battle of Trafalgar, in which engagement he was severely wounded. His figure occupies a prominent position in the celebrated picture of West, "The Death of Nelson". He received his commission in 1807, subsequently served with great bravery on the Solebay, and commanded the Marines, with whom he was a universal favourite, at the capture of Fort St. Louis, Senegal. The expedition with which he was then entrusted was attended with imminent peril to all engaged; and to his honour it ought to be recorded that, it was owing to his keen foresight and prompt representation of the importance of that African stronghold, that the attack was first contemplated, and it was chiefly in consequence of his personal bravery and that of his faithful band of Marines, that the fort was taken. He was left in charge of the fort which he successfully garrisoned, for seven months, during which time nearly half of his men fell victim to the fevers endemic to that region. He afterwards served on board the MINERVA frigate, on a voyage of discovery. His practical talent and scientific attainments rendered him an acquisition to the safety and success of the expedition. After passing through conflicts and dangers seldom equalled in the history of one man, he retired on half pay. In 1820 he came to the Isle of Man, and the following year he married into one of the oldest and most respected Manx families. Since then he has resided in Douglas, where, by his nobleness of mind, heart and life, he gained the esteem of all with whom he came in contact, and has left a lasting memorial of his true worth in the respect and attachment of a very large circle of friends who regret his departure from among them.

WILLIAM RIDDICK

In the 1860s, Mr James Gibson engaged in transcribing many memorial stones in Liverpool churchyards; his notes are now in the records office at Liverpool, (bound into nine volumes with an index). He also wrote a weekly column in the *Liverpool Mercury* entitled *Gleanings from Liverpool Churchyards.* He chose the most interesting inscriptions for his column, and in December, 1884, the following incomplete inscription appeared, taken from a gravestone in the Scotch Kirk, in Oldham, Liverpool:

.... of Colvend in the stewartry of Kirkudbright and late of Liverpool. He was Master's Mate of the Zealous, in the Battle of the Nile, and received a silver medal as a token that he had done his duty to the satisfaction of the Great Nelson. He died 12th February 1808 in the 45th year of his age.

In his column he went on to say: 'the upper part of this stone is decayed, and the name is obliterated. Perhaps some reader may be able to give the name of this memorable seaman'. On January 10th, some weeks later, Mr James Murdock, of Kippford, Scotland, wrote to say the stone was that of William Riddick, his uncle; he confirmed that Riddick was master's mate of the *Zealous* (74) at the Battle of the Nile, and had received a silver medal (the Davison Medal) for his good conduct. He had died at his house in Strand Street, Liverpool, on February 12th 1808. Unfortunately his log of the Battle of the Nile had been burnt and the medal was missing.

Prior to his career in the Royal Navy from 1794 to 1801, it seems Riddick was in the merchant service. He entered the Royal Navy on August 5th 1794 on board the *Enterprise* (28) which was moored in the Thames by the Tower. William entered as a volunteer and able-seaman. After a few days he transferred to the *Sandwich,* a guardship dealing with large numbers of recruits. Ten days later, on August 15th 1794, we find William on the muster book of HMS *Zealous*, listed as an able-seaman. His age was given as 28, and place of birth Leith (this was incorrect).

On September 12th 1794 he was promoted to master's mate, and it was at this rank that he fought at the Nile. The log book for the *Zealous* (Records Office reference number ADM 51/1283) for the period covering the Battle of the Nile makes no mention of William; the entries are brief and condensed but the accounts of action are interesting. The day after the main action, *Zealous* was in pursuit of two French ships and it was reported that seaman George Willis was killed. Admiralty records show that most of the ship's company of HMS *Zealous* were transferred to HMS *Courageux* (74) in May, 1800. William Riddick appears in the muster book of this ship on May 4th 1800. His age is given as 34 and birthplace, (now correct) given as Colvend, County Galloway.

In August, 1800, he was discharged to the Naval Hospital, Haslar, (disease or injury not stated). After some weeks, William was released from Haslar and sent to HMS *Triumph* (74) arriving on board on September 27th. Twelve days later on October 9th, he was transferred to the *Ville de Paris* (110) and then from her on October 21st to the *Courageux*. His stay on this ship was short, and on January 7th 1801, he was moved to the *Venerable* (74) with about 30 others from his ship. Details of his entry into HMS *Venerable* were given as before, with age and place of birth correct.

In November 1801, William, along with others, was discharged as 'unserviceable' (no details given). The pay book of *Venerable* shows all unserviceable men were paid off at Portsmouth, on November 20th 1801.

After his discharge from the Royal Navy, William made his way to the port of Liverpool, and took service in the merchant marine. Riddick made his home in Liverpool, and was one of the Scotch Presbyterians who, along with Mr Gladstone, formed a society to raise funds for the erection of a Scotch Kirk in the city.

By this time, William was not a well man. He had made a will on January 31st 1808 just 13 days before his death. This will is signed with a mark, as it seems he must have been too ill even to sign his name. Although William was not married he had many relations, some in Liverpool. In his will he mentioned his sister, Grizelle, his brother Charles, and others including a younger brother Andrew. He bequeathed a silver watch to Samuel Murdoch, and his quadrant, bed and bedding to James Murdoch. He nominated and appointed the Reverend William Kirkpatrick, Minister of the Scotch Kirk and John Edgan, the Kirk's accountant, as his executors.

It was in the little graveyard of the Scotch Kirk that he was laid to rest, although sadly not for long. As the city grew around the Kirk, people moved out to the suburbs, and the Kirk was used less and less. It was finally closed in about 1919, when the land was purchased by a garage company for redevelopment. The Kirk was pulled down, and the mortal remains of the 450 Scotch Presbyterians buried there were indiscriminately dug up and moved to Everton Cemetery, one of the new municipal burial places found necessary for a growing city. No record of the reinterments was kept, although we have been able to find the general area where the Scotch Presbyterians were placed. We have even found the memorial stones of some from the Kirk in Oldham Street, although unfortunately William's was not amongst them.

LEWIS ROTELEY

Roteley became second lieutenant Royal Marines in 1805 and served in the *Victory* at Trafalgar in this capacity. It is interesting to note that both the headstone of Reeves and the obituary of Roteley claim to be that of the last surviving *Victory* officer from Trafalgar; in fact Reeves lived 12 days longer than Roteley, and Westphall 14 years longer.

In 1808 Roteley became first lieutenant, serving in the *Cleopatra* (32) at the capture of Martinique in 1809. He commanded a detachment of marines at the capture of the French frigate *Topaze* (40), after an action of 40 minutes near Guadaloupe, in 1809.

After he saved four people from drowning a 'Roteley Scholarship' was founded at the Royal Navy School, Eltham, in his memory. He retired on full pay in 1814, and was awarded a medal and two clasps.

Lieutenant Roteley died at May Hill, Swansea in 1861. His obituary appeared just one day after his fellow marine Reeves died.

The obituary notice, in the *Liverpool Weekly Mercury*, Saturday May 4th 1861, page 7 column 4 reads as follows:

Roteley - April 21, aged 76. At his residence, Mayhill, Swansea, Lieut. Roteley, the last surviving officer of the ship "Victory" of Trafalgar, having fought with Nelson at the memorable engagement at Trafalgar. He was allowed to retire from full pay about 40 years ago and from that time he has enjoyed his pension.

At his death and for some time previously he had in his possession a pair of pantaloons which were worn by the immortal Nelson himself, together with other important relics of that eminent naval commander.

Out of 900 who were on board the Victory at Trafalgar, five only now remain. Lieut. Roteley was born at the Castle Heath Hotel, Neath, Glamorganshire, was educated at a school near

Bristol, married Miss Duncombe, daughter of the eminent engineer of that name, by whom he had issue, one surviving daughter; Died at Swansea as stated and his remains were intered with those of his wife and his mother, in the family vault at St Mary's Church, Swansea.

The immediate area of the church was badly damaged during the Second World War, however Roteley's headstone survives and is now sited against the church wall. It reads:

SACRED TO THE MEMORY OF
LEWIS ROTELEY
MAJOR IN THE FOREIGN SERVICE
FIRST LIEUTENANT ROYAL MARINES
WHO DIED APRIL 21st 1861 AGED 76 YEARS
HE SERVED IN THE FLAG SHIP "VICTORY"
UNDER LORD NELSON AT THE BATTLE OF TRAFALGAR
AND WAS SEVERELY WOUNDED BUT KEPT THE DECK
AND SUCCEEDED TO THE COMMAND OF THE REMNANT
OF THE DETACHMENT OF MARINES LEFT ALIVE IN
THE SHIP ON THAT DAY.
ENGAGED IN ACTIVE SERVICE DURING THE WAR
OF 1805 AND FOR FIVE SUCCEEDING YEARS

A SOLDIER WHO WITH NELSON FOUGHT
THE VICTORY SO DEARLY BOUGHT
NOW THE RACE OF LIFE HAS RUN
WITH HIM MAY HOPE HIS 'DUTY'S DONE'.

ALSO IN AFFECTIONATE REMEMBRANCE
OF HIS WIFE ELIZABETH DUNCOMBE ROTELEY
AND OF ELIZABETH ROTELEY, HIS MOTHER
ALSO JANE DOUGLAS ROTELEY
DAUGHTER OF THE ABOVE
WHO DIED FEB.Y 28th 1896

JOHN RUDALL

Born in 1753, the Reverend John Rudall became Vicar of Crediton Church, Devon in 1793. Leaving a curate in charge, he joined the Navy as chaplain in 1799. In 1801 at the battle of Copenhagen he found himself in the remarkable situation of being present in the same ship, the *Edgar* (under Captain Murray) as his three sons, James, William and J Rudall. The *Edgar* (74) led the van and received such heavy fire that 31 men were killed, and 111 wounded, a fifth of the total British casualties in the battle.

The Reverend Rudall was next appointed to the *Royal Sovereign* (100) on August 12th 1805 and was chaplain in her at Trafalgar. Yet again his ship led the van, and again his three sons were present: William a midshipman, James a purser and J Rudall a midshipman aboard the *Defiance* (74). Midshipman J Rudall became lieutenant in 1806 and drowned off Brest on November 26th 1809, as lieutenant of the *Armada* (74) whilst trying to save the life of a marine when boarding the French privateer *Glaveuse*.

The Reverend Rudall left the Navy in 1806 and returned to his church at Crediton, where he remained until his death there in 1835. He is buried at the church, where there is a fine memorial to him which reads:

> **Sacred to the memory of**
> **the Rev. John Rudall**
> **14 years Assistant Minister, and 43 years Vicar of**
> **this parish.**
> **He departed this life Sept. 7th 1835, aged 82**
> **As a tribute of reverential affection, this Tablet**
> **is erected by his surviving children**
> **who here record also**
> **the memory of a beloved Mother**
> **Susanna Rudall wife of the above**
> **She died March 5th 1845 aged 84.**

The father of the present Vicar, Reverend Geering, worked in Portsmouth dockyard for many years and was present during repairs to the *Victory* in the late 1950s.

JOHN ALEXANDER SCOTT

The son of a naval lieutenant and nephew of an admiral, Scott was educated at Charterhouse and St John's Cambridge, where he took a BA and was ordained at the age of 21.

Whilst serving as chaplain to the *Berwick* (74) he was introduced to Nelson for the first time. In 1795 he became Admiral Parker's secretary and chaplain. At the Battle of Copenhagen his linguistic skills were of great value. He spoke French, German, Italian, Spanish, Latin, Greek and now he began to learn Danish and Russian.

After the battle he joined Nelson in the *St George* (98) and assisted in the complicated peace arrangements that followed. He accompanied Nelson to the *Victory* where his knowledge of languages came to the fore: when enemy prizes were taken, he translated despatches and acted as interpreter. He dined with Nelson and was continually in his company, and was with him when he died, supporting him and rubbing his chest to relieve the pain.

Nelson left Scott £200 in his will, but like many others in Nelson's life, once their Chief was gone they found themselves sadly neglected by King and Country.

Reverend Scott left the Navy in 1805 and held the living for Southminster. He rebuilt the chancel in the church there and set a sundial on the wall. He persuaded the people to raise funds to help the families of those who fell at Trafalgar, and framed lists of their names which he hung in the vestry. Scott also left to the church a chart table, bureau and Nelson's mirror from the *Victory*.

In June 1816, the Prince Regent offered him the Crown Living of Catterick, Yorkshire on the recommendation of Lord Liverpool; he became King's Chaplain in November 1817.

When at Catterick, he became good friends with Lady Tyrconnel at Kiplin Hall near Richmond, Yorkshire. George Calvert, who first built the Hall, was the founder of the State of Maryland, USA. Scott gave to Lady Tyrconnel a Morgan and Saunders' metamorphic chair which unfolds into a set of steps, and a pair of Bibles, both from the *Victory*. The Bibles are signed by Nelson and are on view in the library. To the rear of the grounds is an area called 'Nelson Plantation'.

Scott's daughter married Alfred Gatty, Vicar of Ecclesfield 1839-1903, and it was here that he died in 1840, aged 72. He is buried in St Mary's churchyard, Ecclesfield, close to the bottom of the old vicarage garden. A table top tomb reads in part:

> **Waiting for the adoption**
> **the redemption of our body**
> **Here lie buried**
> **Alexander John Scott D.D.**
> **Vicar of Catterick and Southminster**
> **and Chaplain to Admiral Lord Nelson**
> **on board H.M.S. Victory at Trafalgar**
> **He died July 24 1840 aged 72**
> **Also his daughter.**

That Nelson thought highly of Scott is clear, and after Trafalgar, Scott's opinion of his Admiral can be seen in a letter he wrote from the *Victory* to a friend in England:

> *Men are not always themselves and put on*
> *their behaviour with their clothes, but if*
> *you live with a man on board a ship for*
> *years; if you are continually with him in*
> *his cabin, your mind will soon find out*
> *how to appreciate him. I could for ever*
> *tell you the qualities of this beloved man.*
> *I have not shed a tear for years before the*
> *21st October and since, whenever alone,*
> *I am quite like a child.*

WILLIAM SNELL

Commander Snell was born in Antigua in 1790. He was the brother of John Coxetter Snell, master's mate of the *Thunderer* (74) who was listed wounded.

William Snell entered the service in 1799 at the age of nine, and was midshipman aboard the *Britannia* (100) at Trafalgar, under Admiral Northesk, who was third in command of the British fleet.

The *Britannia* was the fourth ship in the line led by Nelson and suffered 52 killed and wounded. She had previously been at the Battle of St Vincent, captained by Foley. Snell became master's mate in 1808 and lieutenant in 1811. After serving in the *Centaur* (74) at the defence of Tarragona, Commander Snell eventually retired in 1853. He received a medal and Trafalgar clasp, and died at his home 'Wood Park', Windle Hill near Neston, Cheshire. This fine Georgian house on the A540 road was purchased in 1959 by Liverpool University, and stands in large grounds.

The *Liverpool Mercury* ran an obituary, on Saturday June 16th, page 2 column 8 which read:

> *June 8 at Woodpark, Neston aged 70. Commander*
> *WILLIAM SNELL R.N. Deceased was one of the few*
> *survivors of the glorious battle of Trafalgar.*

He was buried on June 11th 1860 in the churchyard of St Mary and St Helen, Neston, Cheshire. A flat stone inscription reads:

SACRED
to the
Memory
of
WILLIAM SNELL
Comr. R.N.
of
Wood Park
who died 8th June 1860
AGED 70

This churchyard is of some interest to Nelson enthusiasts as it is also the burial place of one Henry Lyon, Emma Hamilton's father, who died in June 1765, one month after Emma's baptism. His grave is not marked, nor is there any record of where he may lie, which is not unusual for the time.

In Victorian times the church was renovated, and only the tower of the original building remains. Recently the old font was discovered in the tower and was brought back into use. It is of octagonal design with carved leaves upon its sides. This font is almost certainly the one in which the then Emy Lyon, later to become Lady Emma Hamilton, was baptised in May 1765. The cottage where she was born still stands in the village of Ness nearby.

SAMUEL SPENCER

Born at Halifax, Lieutenant Spencer entered the Navy in 1796. He became midshipman in 1797 and was in the *Active* (38) in 1801 in operations off Egypt. In 1803 he was master's mate of the *Maidstone* (32) which was involved in the pursuit of a French privateer, and was in a boat attack on a convoy at La Vandour in 1804. Spencer was master's mate of the *Victory* at Trafalgar in 1805, and he was made lieutenant in 1806. He later served as agent for the Admiralty's Transport Service. He received a medal and two clasps.

He lived in No 3, Grange Vale, Birkenhead, Merseyside which is directly opposite Nelson Road. Lieutenant Spencer suffered three months of paralysis and chest dropsy before he died on December 19th 1850 and was buried in St Mary's, Birkenhead, near the Priory.

In 1956 Cammel Laird's shipyard extended one of their docks to accommodate Naval ships, and St Mary's churchyard lay in its proposed site. Lieutenant Spencer therefore shifted berth to Landican Cemetery, Wirral, together with his flat stone of some weight, where he lies today, in the St Mary's reinterment area, Section S row 5, near the hedge and trees. We would like to thank the Registrar of Landican Cemetery for allowing us to do some serious 'gardening' in order to find and level Lieutenant Spencer's stone which reads:

SACRED
to the memory of
SAMUEL SPENCER ESQ.
Lieut. R.N.
who departed this life
Decr. 19th 1850
Aged 71 years
also
CHARLOTTE MATILDA SPENCER
second daughter of the above
who departed this life
March 6th 1870

FREDERIC THESIGER

Frederic Thesiger first went to sea as a boy with the East India Company and later joined the Royal Navy. He was Rodney's ADC at the Battle of the Saintes, and at the conclusion of the 1778 war with France he joined the Russian Navy.

In 1789 he commanded a Russian 74 and distinguished himself in the war against Sweden, forcing the Swedish Admiral to surrender. The Empress of Russia, Catherine, awarded him a sword of honour and the insignia of the Order of St George.

After Catherine's death, Thesiger became dissatisfied with the new Czar and resigned his commission. Czar Paul refused him his passport and it took Thesiger a year to escape to England. Lord Spencer employed him in the fleet that was to fight at Copenhagen, but Parker was reluctant to make use of Thesiger's local knowledge and ability to speak Russian and Danish. Nelson, however, had no such inhibitions. During the course of the battle, Thesiger volunteered to take peace terms over to the Danes. Carrying a flag of truce, he was rowed over during the height of the action. His command of the language helped save many lives that day, as terms were agreed, and Admiral Parker was recalled home leaving Nelson in command.

Southey reveals an insight into Thesiger's nature in his *Life of Nelson*: 'One day, being accosted in the street by somebody who mistook him for an acquaintance and addressed him as "Smith", Sir Frederic drew himself up and said with awful hauteur, "Sir, do I look like a person of the name of Smith?" '

He died at Elson, near Rowner, Hampshire on August 20th 1805 and was buried in Rowner churchyard. His memorial inscription reads:

SIR FREDERICK THESIGER
Late of the R.N. & Agent for Prisoners of war
at the depot of Portsmouth. Died 20th August 1805
Aged 47

EDMUND FANNING THOMAS

Commander Thomas was promoted to lieutenant in 1798. At Trafalgar he served as second lieutenant in the *Bellerophon* (74) and acted as first when Captain Cooke was killed. He retired in 1830 as commander and died at Cleethorpes, near Grimsby, on April 28th 1842.

He was buried at the Old Clee parish churchyard and the local family history group, having surveyed this churchyard, have a revised list of the stones. Commander Thomas' inscription was first listed at the turn of the century, and it states:

> *EDMUND FANNING THOMAS*
> *COMMANDER R.N.*
> *born 4th Sept. 1778 died 28th April 1842*
> *and of his widow Frances Thomas*
> *born 24th April 1782 died 30th March 1858*

There is a second stone which reads:

> *FRANCES MARY THOMAS*
> *died 8th August 1811*
> *aged 3 years 2 months*

WILLIAM TURNER

William Turner was a corporal of the marines aboard the *Victory* at Trafalgar and was stationed at one of the guns on the quarter-deck during the battle.

After the war in 1815 he continued his trade as a locksmith for a Mr Bolton in Warrington for many years, before setting up on his own.

On June 3rd 1868 he wrote a letter to the *Warrington Guardian* which reads as follows:

> *ANOTHER TRAFALGAR SAILOR. -- To the Editor. -- Sir, I have seen the notices which have appeared in the newspapers relating to the late decease of Lieutenant Pollard, who was Lord Nelson's signal-midshipman at the battle of Trafalgar, and as I was a marine on board the same ship, the Victory, and an older man than Lieutenant Pollard, my friends have urged me to send to your page of Notes and Queries a short notice of myself, who am an old resident of the town, not with a view of obtaining any recognition of my former services, but simply to say that I am still living here, aged 87 years, able and willing to work at my trade of a locksmith, and very proud to serve any lady or gentleman who may call for my services in this line of business. This I say on the word of honour of an old saltwater "Jack." I am the marine "who did his duty, and is ready to do it again." I was born at Chester in the year 1781, but at four years old went with my parents to Wolverhampton, where I stayed until I was 20 years of age learning the trade of a locksmith. In the latter part of 1799, I enlisted in the marines, and remained with them until 1815, so that I served during the whole war, with the exception of a few months during the short Peace of Amiens. At the battle of Trafalgar I was stationed at the first gun on the quarter-deck of Lord Nelson's ship, the Victory, and whilst waiting for an opportunity when we could send a shot which would do some execution, I saw Lord Nelson, with other officers, walking on the other side*

of the quarter-deck. When he was wounded, I saw his lordship stagger, and he was caught in the arms of a sergeant of marines, whose name was Secker. I saw Lord Nelson carried off the deck, and before the action was over, I was told that he was dead. The flag was lowered half-mast down before the close of the action. I have a very clear recollection of the battle of Trafalgar, more especially with regard to my own ship and officers, and as your paper has a wide circulation, I shall be very happy to reply to any inquiries which may be made - WILLIAM TURNER, locksmith, Mill-street, Warrington, 3rd June, 1868.

William Turner died on November 7th 1869 of old age at his home 16 Mill Street, Warrington, aged 88. He was buried in Warrington Cemetery, Manchester Road, on November 10th by the Reverend John Ingle Dredge, according to entry B4319 in the burial register. He lies in consecrated ground Section D No 659, together with his wife. There is an upright York stone which simply reads:

WILLIAM TURNER

DIED 7th NOVEMBER 1869
AGED 88 YEARS

JANE HIS WIFE DIED NOVEMBER 1st
1863 AGED 64 YEARS

THOMAS TURNER

DIED 24th JULY 1876
AGED 61 YEARS.

JAMES ROBERTSON WALKER

Born James Robertson in 1783 at Letterewe, Ross-shire to James Robertson JP and Annabella Mackenzie, he entered the Navy in 1801 and served in the *Canopus* (80) off Cadiz in 1803-04.

At Trafalgar he was one of the midshipmen aboard the *Victory*. In 1806 in the *Thames* (32) he was present at the attempt of the destruction of the Boulogne flotilla by rockets. He was in the *Bellisle* (74) at the reduction of the islands of St Thomas and St Croix in 1807, and was acting lieutenant of the *Fawn* (18) at the taking of a privateer and three merchant vessels under the Puerto Rico batteries in 1808.

After continuing as acting lieutenant of the *Hazard* (16) at the capture of the French frigate *Topaze* (40) and the reduction of Martinique, he was made lieutenant in 1809. He was mentioned in despatches while serving in the *Hazard* for the destruction of a French privateer at the capture of Guadaloupe in 1810, and the capture of several American vessels from 1812-13, plus the privateer *Eleanor* whilst in the *Antelope* (50) in 1813.

In 1814 he succeeded to the command of the *Confiance* (37) and in the action with the US squadron under Macdonough in 1814, was unfortunately captured. He was tried by Court Martial and fully exonerated, and promoted commander the following year. As a reserve captain, he was awarded a medal with three clasps in 1851, and he died in 1858.

James Robertson had taken his wife's name Walker upon their marriage.

He was buried in a vault in Distington churchyard, Cumbria, at the Holy Spirit Church. His memorial reads as follows:

Erected by Katherine Robertson Walker
in memory of her husband
James Robertson Walker Esquire
of Gilgarron - Captain R.N.

born at Letterewe, Ross-shire 22 June 1783
died at Gilgarran 26th October 1858.

He was on board the Victory at the battle of
Trafalgar and died during a brilliant career.
Served his country faithfully.
Beloved and respected, he died in the joyful
hope of a glorious resurrection.

JOHN COBB WHICHER

Reverend Whicher served as Chaplain in *HMS Achilles* at Trafalgar. He joined the Navy two years after he was appointed Rector of Stopham, Pulborough, Sussex.

He was apparently related to the Barttelot family who had the gift of the living of the parish, and therefore he was able to resume his duties as Rector after his Naval service was complete.

The above information is from the family papers of Colonel W Barttelot and *The Sea Chaplains* by Gordon Taylor.

There is a memorial tablet on the north side of the chancel arch which reads:

Sacred to the memory
of the
Rev'd John Cobb Whicher
Rector of this parish
45 years
He departed this life
March 12th 1841
Aged 69 years

His grave is outside under the south-east wall, and his headstone reads:

Rev'd John Cobb Whicher
Obit March 12th 1841